1979

Foundations of Modern History

Foundations of Modern History*
already published

Britain and Europe in the Seventeenth Century   *J. R. Jones*

Crisis of Empire:
Great Britain and the American Colonies 1754–1783   *I. R. Christie*

The Government of Elizabethan England   *A. G. R. Smith*

Artisans and San-Culottes:
Popular Movements in France and Britain during the French Revolution
Gwyn A. Williams

England in the Eighteen Thirties:
Decade of Reform   *Geoffrey B. A. M. Finlayson*

Origins of the First World War   *L. C. F. Turner*

Arms, Autarky and Aggression:
A Study in German Foreign Policy 1933–1939   *William Carr*

The Economics of European Imperialism   *Alan Hodgart*

British Appeasement in the 1930s   *William R. Rock*

Neutrality or Commitment:
The Evolution of Dutch Foreign Policy 1667–1795   *Alice Clare Carter*

* A. Goodwin, Emeritus Professor of Modern History, University of Manchester, was General Editor of this series until his retirement from the position in 1975.

British Appeasement in the 1930s

William R. Rock

W · W · Norton & Company · Inc ·

New York

Printed in the United States of America.
All Rights Reserved
First Edition

Library of Congress Cataloging in Publication Data
Rock, William R
  British appeasement in the 1930s.
  (Foundations of modern history)
  Bibliography: p.
  Includes index.
  1. Great Britain—Foreign relations—Germany.
2. Germany—Foreign relations—Great Britain.
3. Great Britain—Foreign relations—1936-1945.
4. Great Britain—Politics and government—1936-1945.
5. Chamberlain, Neville, 1869-1940.   I.   Title
DA47.2.R63   327.41′043   77-17549
ISBN 0-393-05668-6
ISBN 0-393-09060-4 pbk.

1 2 3 4 5 6 7 8 9 0

Contents

General Preface

This study of the rise and fall of the British policy of 'appeasement' in the inter-war period by one of America's leading authorities deserves a wide and discerning audience. The handling of so complex and controversial a theme calls for the exercise of the special qualities of impartiality, sympathy, and balanced judgement in which some British historians have, in their treatment of the subject, shown themselves deficient. Professor Rock's dispassionate assessment will supply the present generation of students with what it really needs if it is not to be misled by the legacy of pre-war controversies or by the pejorative associations of the term itself. His present work provides, first, an explanation of the political, economic and military factors which prompted the evolution of a policy designed above all to safeguard European peace by the progressive alleviation of German grievances arising from the Versailles settlement, but subsequently inflamed by Hitler. Secondly, it exhibits a sympathetic and informed understanding of the collective anti-war mentality of the British people, at a time of post-war disillusionment, contracting economic horizons, waning international influence, and the anticipated complete vulnerability of the civilian population to German air attack. It was, indeed, this disposition which did so much to palliate, if not to condone, the pursuit of appeasement even after it had ceased to be consonant with international security, the independent exitence of Austria and Czechoslovakia, and the vital interests of Britain and its allies. Thirdly, the author gives a fair but clinical estimate of Neville Chamberlain's own personal responsibility, as prime minister, for the original conception of the policy of 'active' appeasement and his stubborn adherence to it in the face of repeated setbacks and tragic failure.

The treatment throughout is analytical and this allows the case for and against appeasement to be discussed in detail as it was presented by its contemporary advocates and critics and as it now appears after the lapse of a generation.

Above all, however, Professor Rock's account will be welcomed for its mastery of the voluminous first-hand evidence and of recent specialist research and its convincing evaluation of the policy of appeasement in its historical perspective. Before the advent of Chamberlain to the premiership appeasement was 'passive', 'exploratory' and, in general, justifiable, in the sense that it seemed to afford a viable alternative to the increasingly heavy financial burdens of rearmament. In Chamberlain's hands, however, the policy became a personal and almost fanatical 'mission', steadily pursued, in a devious and authoritarian manner, by a man not noted for his knowledge of foreign affairs, and naive in his estimate of the willingness of the dictators to compromise or even keep their agreements. Chamberlain's circumvention of his own cabinet colleagues, such as Eden, of senior foreign office officials, such as Vansittart, and even of the dictators themselves, made his political methods as unedifying as they were inept. The main indictment of his policy, however, must turn not only on its inadequacy and ultimate failure, but also on Chamberlain's utter lack of the 'realism' and shrewd judgement, which he foolishly claimed for himself and denied to his critics. It is interesting to observe that Professor Rock is, nevertheless, prepared to admit that the Munich agreement was itself defensible, while he condemns Chamberlain's own ludicrous and specious eulogy of it as 'Peace with Honour' and his obsessional defence of the policy of appeasement even when it lay in ruins.

A. GOODWIN

Preface

Much has been written on various aspects of British appeasement in the 1930s. The British government's efforts to implement the policy, especially in relation to Nazi Germany, have been thoroughly chronicled. The origins of the policy have been traced and some of the major forces behind it have been analysed. The chief supporters of the policy, as well as its primary opponents, have been identified and examined; the course of debate over the policy (both at the time and later) has been studied. The Munich agreement, often taken, rather erroneously, as the sum and substance of appeasement, has been described and evaluated in dozens of books and articles. Judgements about appeasement, particularly its relationship to the coming of the Second World War, have been widely formulated and freely proffered. Why, then, still another book on appeasement?

The answer is a simple one. There is clearly a need to bring together in a single volume of modest proportions the varied facets of the subject which have been treated in numerous specialized studies, to present them succinctly with some analytical overview, and to incorporate recent scholarship into the general interpretation of appeasement. These are the things that this little volume purports to do.

I am grateful for the support and encouragement which I received in the preparation of this work from colleagues in the history department at Bowling Green State University, especially Professors Gary Hess and Bernard Sternsher, and the members of my family—my wife, Suzanne, as well as Steve (who proof-read), Anne, and Brian, daily inquirers about my progress. I also acknowledge with gratitude the work of two efficient typists, Mrs Nedra Bradley and Mrs Jo Mahoney.

WILLIAM R. ROCK

1 Neville Chamberlain and the Pursuit of Appeasement

Neville Chamberlain was, in the years 1937–39, a prime minister with a mission. The mission was somehow to arrive at a general settlement of differences with an increasingly truculent and aggressive Germany in order to strengthen peace and promote stability in Europe. The policy he developed, partly on the precedents of his predecessors and partly anew, was called appeasement. It has since become one of the most controversial, and vilified, policies in the history of international relations.

The German problem was an old one. The basic grievances which Nazi leadership, since 1933, had been exploiting were in large part the legacy of the First World War and the much maligned Treaty of Versailles (1919). British prime ministers of the 1920s had confronted the problem too, and their varying efforts to reduce its dimensions had met with some modest success, despite the reluctance of France to make concessions of note to the former German enemy. But the emergence of Nazism in Germany in the early 1930s, as a result of powerful forces coalesced by the world-wide depression which began in 1929, gave a new intensity to the German problem. Whereas German statesmen of the 1920s were of necessity compelled to seek the adjustment of grievances by means of continuous diplomatic prodding, and occasionally passive resistance, quite apart from the threat of force, which they in fact did not possess, Nazi leadership introduced a new strand in German diplomacy. Cautiously at first, but with increasing audacity as the months passed by and confidence grew, they reiterated unmet demands, developed a military machine to give force to their words, and revealed their intention to compel revision of Versailles.

The policy evolved by the Baldwin government in the mid-1930s for dealing with the growing threat from Germany was one perhaps best described as 'wait and see' or 'cunctation', as Vansittart[1] labelled it. Hoping for an Anglo-German détente based on modest overtures which owed their substance to the Locarno arrangement of 1925, but acknowledging the need for rearmament, and especially an air deterrent, British policy-makers 'hovered uneasily between the doctrine of the free hand and the historic principle of the balance of power in

---

[1] Robert Vansittart, permanent under secretary in the foreign office.

Europe'.[2] Availing themselves unassumingly of the few occasions which offered an opportunity to deal with Germany, they formulated no plan of action and took little real initiative—a likely reflection of the uncertainties surrounding the re-emergence of Germany as a power in Europe as well as Baldwin's aversion to foreign affairs generally and his preoccupation with other matters.

Chamberlain doubted the adequacy of this approach for some time before he became prime minister, and when he assumed leadership in May 1937, was determined to take a more positive stance.[3] As chancellor of the exchequer (1932–37) he had been especially concerned about the growing expense of rearmament and its impact on the domestic economy and social programme of the government. He thus devised a thesis that defence, diplomacy, and economic vitality were all part of a single question, and where economic resilience was threatened by the demands of defence, diplomacy must assume the burden. In this way he came to the view that diplomatic action could, and should, reduce the need for costly rearmament, thus averting unsettling disturbances in the domestic economy. This basic strategy was directly responsible for the policy he pursued with utmost diligence for the next two years.[4]

Chamberlain's first objective was to come to terms with Germany. The aggressive actions of Italy (in Abyssinia and Spain) and Japan (in China) were also disconcerting, but Germany was the key. Beyond the facts of her strength and potential, her obvious centrality to European stability and her intense dissatisfaction as the victim of Versailles, the re-establishment of cordial Anglo-German relations would neutralize the danger from Italy and significantly reduce her pomposity. It might also open the way for a firmer stance toward Japan, though much depended in this regard on the role which the United States was prepared to play. Only when Chamberlain's initial approaches to Germany failed to elicit a positive response did Italy loom larger in his calculations and he begin to think about weakening Germany's position by wooing Italy from her, or at the very least, using Italy's good offices for the purpose of influencing Berlin. And appeasement, in its positive European connotation, was never really tried on Japan. Britain's policy in east Asia, especially after the Sino-Japanese War had begun, constituted in essence an attempted benevolent neutrality which tended to favour China.[5]

The obstacles to Anglo-German understanding were essentially of

[2] Keith Middlemas, *Diplomacy of Illusion: the British Government and Germany, 1937–1939* (London, 1972), p. 17.

[3] Chamberlain often confessed his 'inability' to confront a problem without seeking directly to solve it.

[4] See Middlemas, *Diplomacy of Illusion*, pp. 32–59.

[5] The British had earlier acknowledged their inability to counter Japan alone, and were engaged in what might best be described as a 'holding action' in the Far East. After the outbreak of the Sino-Japanese War, Chamberlain apparently did not think seriously about conciliatory approaches to Japan, as he had in 1934. Neither he nor his colleagues pressed in the cabinet or the foreign policy committee for a policy of appeasement in East Asia. Indeed, Chamberlain did not assume a leading role in the formulation of East Asian policy. This was left, to a surprising degree,

two kinds—injustices remaining from Versailles and mistrust in the minds of both peoples. Since the democracies were responsible for the peace settlement, it followed that they must take the lead and make the first concessions in the effort to right past wrongs and rebuild mutual confidence. Britain was not, of course, the sole author of Versailles. But in view of French instability and American isolationism, Chamberlain was quite prepared to proceed alone. Thus the issues of economic appeasement (the hope of exploring expanded Anglo-German economic cooperation and of demonstrating to Germany that her economic objectives could be attained without massive rearmament and the threat of war)[6] and colonial appeasement (the projected return of colonial territories to Germany as a factor in improving relations with her)[7] were widely discussed by British officials during the years 1936–37. Much remained uncertain—the form and nature of specific proposals, which colonies to return, the timing and conditions of British 'offers', the cooperation of France, indeed the extent of German interest—but there emerged from protracted debate a broad affirmative consensus, with the idea that colonial appeasement in particular should be explored at an early, convenient moment.[8] Chamberlain was optimistic about the prospects, though he tended to view the actual transfer of colonies as the culmination, not the starting point, of détente with Germany. These matters were doubtless in the back of his mind when, shortly after succeeding Baldwin, he invited the German foreign minister to visit London.

Von Neurath accepted, then declined on a pretext connected with the Spanish Civil War. Shortly thereafter, the foreign policy committee of the cabinet duly noted (June 28th) that there was no immediate hope for appeasement.[9] Nor were the ensuing contacts made by Nevile

---

to the permanent officials of the foreign office, who were sympathetic to the Chinese and very reluctant to countenance concessions to Tokyo. These conclusions emerge from the thorough study by Bradford A. Lee, *Britain and the Sino-Japanese War, 1937–1939: a Study in the Dilemmas of British Decline* (Stanford, 1973). Other useful works on British policy in East Asia are William Roger Louis, *British Strategy in the Far East, 1919–1939* (Oxford, 1971) and Ann Trotter, *Britain and East Asia, 1933–1937* (New York, 1975).

[6] Economic appeasement, often ignored in studies of British foreign policy under Chamberlain, was an important element between 1937 and 1939. For a short account, see C. A. MacDonald, 'Economic Appeasement and the German "Moderates", 1937–1939: an Introductory Essay', *Past & Present*, no. 56 (August, 1972), pp. 105–35. A fuller study is Berndt Jürgen Wendt. *Economic Appeasement: Handel und Finanz in der britischen Deutschland Politik, 1933–1939* (Düsseldorf, 1971). See also Martin Gilbert and Richard Gott, *The Appeasers* (London, 1963), pp. 189–97.

[7] On colonial appeasement, see Gilbert and Gott, *The Appeasers*, pp. 90–108; Middlemas, *Diplomacy of Illusion*, pp. 110–15, 141–3; and Ian Colvin, *The Chamberlain Cabinet* (London, 1971), pp. 42–3.

[8] Anthony Eden, the foreign secretary, had serious reservations; it was over this issue that he and Chamberlain had one of their earliest clashes.

[9] This committee was formed after Germany's march into the Rhineland in 1936. Composed of six to nine ministers, it was a convenient place for the secret discussion of foreign policy. Chamberlain was a member from the beginning. It was in this committee that the policy of appeasement was at length pushed forward. See Colvin, *The Chamberlain Cabinet*, pp. 36–43.

Henderson, newly-appointed ambassador in Berlin, encouraging. There seemed little basis for discussion in the stark alternatives posed by Nazi officials—an Anglo-German division of the world, with Germany paramount in Europe, Britain overseas, or a Germany forced by lack of cooperation to plan the destruction of Britain. But in November a convenient opportunity for testing the idea of appeasement on German leaders arose in the form of an invitation to Halifax, lord president of the council (and master of the Middleton foxhounds), to attend an international hunting exhibition in Berlin.

After Chamberlain had overridden the reservations of Anthony Eden, the foreign secretary, and the foreign office about the wisdom of appearing too eager for German favours, Halifax also journeyed to Berchtesgaden to see Hitler. In a wide ranging conversation characterized by Hitler's sidestepping of meaningful discussion on specific issues, Halifax conveyed his message of British reasonableness in confronting and resolving outstanding questions; he offered colonial rearrangement as part of a general settlement and even spoke of expected alterations in the European order (Danzig, Austria, Czechoslovakia).[10] He returned to London cautiously sanguine about the prospects for Anglo-German understanding. Chamberlain was frankly enthusiastic; a fair basis for discussion had been established and a useful atmosphere created.

But nothing happened in consequence. While the British consulted with French leaders about the details of negotiation with Germany, nothing was heard from Berlin. Subsequent contacts showed the Nazi leaders to be uninterested, even hostile. To less persistent men this would have been most discouraging, but Chamberlain was determined to push on, concerned to demonstrate clearly the seriousness of his intentions in Berlin.

During January 1938, both the foreign policy committee and the full cabinet discussed a paper circulated by Eden entitled 'Further Steps Towards a General Settlement'. The paper outlined in general terms the nature of a settlement with Germany, alternative means of advancing it, and the contribution which Germany might make towards general appeasement. There was obvious confusion about how to proceed. But Chamberlain had an idea and introduced on January 24th a plan for associating Germany with a new form of colonial administration in Africa on a demilitarized and international basis. Henderson was urging colonial settlement first, with a minimum of conditions related to other issues, and his suggestions were receiving serious consideration.

Early February found the foreign policy committee wrestling with instructions to Henderson about approaching Germany on the colonial issue. An early draft provided for German assurances about the independence of Austria and Czechoslovakia. Warnings from von Neurath, however, that such assurances were impossible resulted in revised instructions which only mentioned Austria and Czechoslovakia as

---

[10] For a full analysis, see Lois G. Schwoerer, 'Lord Halifax's Visit to Germany: November 1937', *Historian* xxxii, no. 3 (1970), pp. 353–75.

illustrations of the principle of collaboration. There the matter rested while other events interrupted the pursuit of colonial concessions.

Meanwhile, Chamberlain's confidence in appeasement was apparent in his handling of a proposal in mid-January from President Franklin Roosevelt. The prime minister feared that Roosevelt's idea of calling a world conference in Washington to discuss the underlying causes of international tension would only irritate Germany and Italy and cut across his own efforts to deal with the dictators. Pressed for time and confident of his own judgement, he replied accordingly without consulting Eden, who was vacationing in France. Shocked at what he saw as the cavalier dismissal of an opportunity to bring America's influence to bear in Europe, Eden subsequently secured, through several tense cabinet meetings, a modification of Chamberlain's initial reply. But Roosevelt dropped the matter there. What the president's proposal, with full British backing, might have accomplished must perforce remain uncertain; but its abrupt rejection was clearly instrumental in the estrangement a few weeks later of Eden from Chamberlain and the policy of appeasement.

An exchange of letters between Chamberlain and Mussolini in July 1937 had suggested that the Duce was prepared to discuss all points of difference in Italy's relations with Britain. There had been no immediate follow-up because of Italian belligerence in Abyssinia and Spain and Chamberlain's 'Germany-first' approach to appeasement. But contacts with Mussolini early in February 1938, through Chamberlain's sister-in-law Ivy, an old acquaintance of the Duce, revealed again Italian readiness, now tinged with anxiety in view of Germany's current bullying of Austria, to reach an agreement with Britain. Into this cause Chamberlain threw himself with something resembling reckless abandon. Intent on turning this opportunity to advantage in the cause of appeasement, and seeing it, in fact, as his last chance with Italy, he went to very great lengths, in conversations with the Italian ambassador, Grandi, to accept the Italian view and to agree to negotiations without conditions. In the process he also engaged in questionable tactics to undermine or circumvent the protests of Eden, who believed that, lacking tangible evidence of Italian good faith, neither the timing nor the projected technique of conversations was appropriate. The issue forced to the surface a long-evolving, though mutually muffled, antagonism between prime minister and foreign secretary, a contrariety embracing temperament, outlook, and general political philosophy as well as differences of view on specific policy issues. The upshot was Eden's resignation (February 20th) and Chamberlain's enhanced determination, fortified by the concurrence of most of his cabinet colleagues, to proceed with Italian appeasement as he saw fit.[11]

[11] It was Eden's resignation which brought the validity of appeasement into open public controversy, there to be debated with increasing intensity as long as the policy lasted. See William R. Rock, *Appeasement on Trial: British Foreign Policy and its Critics, 1938–1939* (Hamden, Conn., 1966), pp. 19, 31–45.

Eden's successor at the foreign office, Lord Halifax, was a man of experience, prestige, and irreproachable personal qualities who was wholly attuned to Chamberlain's policy and way of thinking. Steadfastly loyal, and willing to stand aside when the prime minister wished to take the initiative, as he often did, he made an unusually compatible colleague. But he was not completely a puppet; his fits of conscience and his feel for public sentiment occasionally added a material leaven to appeasement.

Halifax had barely taken office when Hitler stunned Europe by annexing Austria (March 12th). There had been ominous forebodings for at least a month. Eden had summarized them for the cabinet on February 16th. Again on March 9th, Halifax reported that Germany appeared 'set head-on to achieve its aims in central Europe' and did not wish to tie her hands by talks.[12] After the event, Chamberlain denounced this typical illustration of power politics which made international appeasement much more difficult to attain, but felt 'this thing had to come.' Nothing short of overwhelming force would have stopped it. At least the matter was out of the way, and the next question was how to prevent a similar course of events in Czechoslovakia.[13]

There had always been in Britain a sentimental conviction that the prohibition of *Anschluss* by the peace treaty of 1919 had been wrong. Thus it was not so much the principle of the union which shocked the British as the brutal way in which it was accomplished. That is what they protested in Berlin and discussed among themselves in the days which followed. Chamberlain acknowledged that conversations with Germany must be laid aside for a time, and that acceleration in rearmament was necessary to demonstrate Britain's determination not to be bullied. But he was hopeful that, if another violent coup in Czechoslovakia could be avoided, which he thought feasible, Europe might settle down again and peace talks be resumed with the Germans. So the independence and integrity of Austria, officially upheld in former years as a vital element in European peace, was waived in the name of appeasement.

The shock of the *Anschluss*, accompanied as it was by anxious expressions of concern for the future in both parliament and press, might reasonably have prompted a serious reappraisal of both policy and strategy. It did not. Rejecting the notion that anything on the European scene had radically changed and proceeding largely without the benefit of considered professional advice from within or consultation abroad, Chamberlain and his colleagues determined not to abandon or modify the policy of appeasement—still essentially untested as a cure for Europe's ills—but to pursue it more assiduously.

With Austria gone, Czechoslovakia at once became the focal point of attention. British policy there was decided in a series of foreign policy

---

[12] Colvin, *The Chamberlain Cabinet*, p. 103.
[13] *ibid.*, pp. 105–6.

committee and cabinet meetings (March 18th–22nd) and announced by Chamberlain, in muted language which hid the contemplated coercion of the Czechs, to the House of Commons on March 24th. It was simple, clear and 'more positive than anything which had been tried out' yet by Chamberlain.[14] Under pressure from Britain and France, Czechoslovakia was to come to terms, whatever they might entail, with its disaffected German minority,[15] thereby removing another German grievance and smoothing the way for Anglo-German understanding. Thus the cabinet embarked in confidence on the road which led to Munich. There were twists and turns in the next six months of travelling, but the destination had been firmly set.

It was necessary to ensure the cooperation of the French, especially in view of their mutual defence alliance with Czechoslovakia. British efforts culminated in a visit to London on April 28th–29th by Daladier, the French premier, and his foreign secretary, Bonnet. The initial assumption that the French, sharing British aspirations for peace and conscious of their military weakness, would quickly and gratefully embrace the British position proved to be only half correct. It took all Chamberlain's persuasive powers, wielded to the point of bullying and belittling, to overcome French reservations and hesitations.[16] The consequences were twofold, one specific and obvious, the other general and subtle: Britain and France would make a joint approach to Prague, while Britain alone approached Berlin, to encourage solution of the Czech problem; and Britain's ascendency in Anglo-French relations, especially as they pertained to a common policy towards the rest of Europe, began to appear.

Meanwhile, Britain had concluded an agreement of sorts with Italy. Conservations begun in Rome on March 8th, through Lord Perth, the British ambassador, resulted in an agreement in mid-April which covered a wide range of conflicting interests. Its practical effect would hinge upon Italian implementation of a British scheme for evacuating 'volunteers' from Spain and Britain's initiative in raising at Geneva the question of recognizing Italian Abyssinia. Chamberlain told the House of Commons, in seeking its approval of the agreement on May 2nd, that the clouds of mistrust and suspicion in Anglo-Italian relations had already cleared away and that a 'new era' had begun for the two nations. His optimism was premature. Unabated expressions of Italian hostility toward Britain, the bombing throughout the summer of British ships in Spanish ports by Italian pilots, and continued Italian violations of the internationally adopted policy of nonintervention in

[14] Middlemas, *Diplomacy of Illusion*, p. 196. Both Middlemas, pp. 182–97, and Colvin, *The Chamberlain Cabinet*, pp. 106–15, trace the formulation of this policy.
[15] Three and a half million Germans who inhabited the Sudetenland on the outer fringes of Czechoslovakia.
[16] Middlemas devotes an entire chapter to 'The Conversion of France', *Diplomacy of Illusion*, pp. 211–41. The extent to which France's demoralization was advanced by Britain's policy of discouragement is both a matter of debate and a subject worthy of further investigation.

the Spanish Civil War precluded any 'settlement of the Spanish problem' (as the conditions which Britain sought soon came to be known) and forced postponement of efforts to implement the agreement until after the Czechoslovak crisis of 1938 had passed.

In the wake of the *Anschluss*, the government acknowledged the need for a fresh review of Britain's defence programme, and there was considerable haggling in the cabinet over issues related to rearmament from mid-March to mid-May. Generally, the lines were drawn between those, the service ministers among them, who favoured increased military preparedness and those, including treasury officials and the prime minister, who saw the nation's economic strength, unthreatened by heavy increases in military expenditure, as her first line of defence. In particular, discussion centred on various schemes for aircraft production, with Lord Swinton, minister for air, pushing hard for significant expansion—and being rewarded in mid-May by Chamberlain's request for his resignation. The upshot was no important change in the tempo of defence preparation and an undiminished reliance on diplomacy to protect the nation.[17]

The unexpected in human events sometimes destroys the best laid plans. The May crisis nearly had that effect on Chamberlain's hopes for settlement by concession in Czechoslovakia. During the third week of May, rumours of German troop movements and a suddenly deteriorating situation in the Sudetenland made it appear that another lightning German coup was impending. The policy of pressuring Prague to get on with the Sudeten German negotiations had already been in operation for several weeks.[18] But it could not succeed if Germany refused to wait. In consequence, the British issued a surprisingly stiff warning to Germany against precipitous action; should a German attack occur, France had obligations to Czechoslovakia and Britain could not guarantee that she herself would stand aside.

This was in essence the warning for which the French had argued, in the face of British intransigence, in London a few weeks earlier. Chamberlain thought it decisive in turning Germany back—a Germany which had now demonstrated how 'utterly untrustworthy and dishonest' it was.[19] But the British warning was a fitful thing, issued on impulse, on Halifax's initiative, in a moment of crisis; it did not herald a new direction in British policy. It was qualified in word and discarded in practice before the week was out. Indeed, the lesson drawn from the crisis by Chamberlain and his colleagues was not that Hitler, in

---

[17] For more detail, see Colvin, *The Chamberlain Cabinet*, pp. 116–26, and Middlemas, *Diplomacy of Illusion*, pp. 216ff.

[18] It was not without effect. Confronted by a Sudeten German party congress decision (Carlsbad, late April) demanding in effect union with Germany and a complete reorientation of Czechoslovak foreign policy, the Czech government was loathe to proceed in view of the new conditions. It relented, however, Anglo-French 'encouragement' undoubtedly influencing its attitude.

[19] Chamberlain writing to his sister. Keith Feiling, *The Life of Neville Chamberlain* (London, 1947), p. 354.

the future, would be restrained by firmness, but that (as effectively stated by F. S. Northedge) 'everything must be done to avoid a repetition of the crisis since next time the outcome would be far more unpleasant.'[20]

Thus the British followed with great interest the course of Czech-Sudeten German negotiations which sputtered along from early June to mid-July. There was in the cabinet growing doubt that a solution of the minority problem would be sufficient to ensure peace. The French and Russian pacts of assistance with Czechoslovakia also seemed a source of trouble, and Halifax began to contemplate readjustments in Czechoslovakia's foreign relations to meet this difficulty. Here potentially was a new refinement in appeasement, asking the aggrieved 'whether he would like concessions which would immensely strengthen his position before he himself had formally proposed them.'[21] But a lack of response from France shelved the idea for a time.

Mid-July witnessed a complete breakdown in Czech-Sudeten German negotiations, leaving a dangerously explosive situation unresolved. In the same month came what appeared to be the most positive response yet from Hitler to British initiatives. The Führer's personal adjutant, Captain Fritz Wiedemann, arrived in London to propose a visit by 'some important German personage', probably Göring, for the purpose of exploring a comprehensive Anglo-German agreement. Halifax, who, with Chamberlain's approval, was the only person to confer with Wiedemann, declared the current moment of tension over Czechoslovakia unpropitious for such a development, but that a Czechoslovak settlement, or a German renunciation of recourse to force in Czechoslovakia, would certainly change the situation.[22]

This combination of events prompted the British to initiate a scheme for mediation in Czechoslovakia which had been contemplated for at least a month. With quick approval from France and the grudging consent of the Czechs, Lord Runciman (lord president of the council) was pressed into service in Prague. An independent conciliator, not a representative of the British government—so Chamberlain carefully explained in the Commons—his job was to hear all the facts and arguments and to suggest expedients and modifications in the demands of both parties. As Sir Samuel Hoare, the home secretary, later conceded, perhaps no one fully realized how the Runciman mission 'inevitably dragged us more deeply into the forefront of the struggle between Germans and Slavs'. Chamberlain saw it as a logical step in his plan to reduce the danger points in Europe and promote appeasement. It

[20] F. S. Northedge, *The Troubled Giant: Britain among the Great Powers, 1916–1939* (London and New York, 1966), p. 510.
[21] *ibid.*, p. 513.
[22] British efforts to follow up this initiative, on the basis of Anglo-German cooperation in promoting a peaceful settlement in Czechoslovakia, elicited no German response. Apparently Wiedemann's visit was only a probe. But the initial British conclusion was that Hitler at last had realized he had much to gain by the use of peaceful means.

did not occur to him that a respected English liberal, confronted with the passions of continental nationalism, 'might have little influence upon a controversy that had already burst into flames'.[23] Nor was there suspicion in London that Hitler would press his cause to the verge of war.

Runciman's efforts throughout the month of August achieved nothing. Czechoslovak willingness to grant anything that would not endanger the nation's integrity and security was ably matched by Sudeten German unwillingness, backed by Hitler, to accept anything short of what Prague apparently would never grant. The latter was particularly disturbing in view of alarming intelligence reports arriving in London from Germany to the effect that Hitler was preparing to move militarily and that only a strong British warning would deter him. Bloody civil disturbances in the Sudetenland and sensational atrocity stories in the German press also boded ill.

There was, understandably, consternation in London about how to proceed. By September 2nd, Runciman saw no solution but a settlement imposed by Britain and Germany. The cabinet pondered a warning to Hitler, but rejected it on the grounds that it was unwise to threaten unless prepared to carry out the threat. It resolved instead to keep Germany guessing as to Britain's ultimate attitude. The 'volley of abuse'[24] which greeted *The Times*'s (September 7th) suggestion that the Sudetenland simply be ceded to Germany seemed to reveal a definite public sentiment against surrender. Thereafter, consultation among principal cabinet ministers and foreign office officials resulted (September 9th) in agreement on a strongly worded message to Berlin declaring that in the event of war Britain would stand by France. But the message was not delivered; Ambassador Henderson's protest that it would merely provoke Hitler won him permission to lay it quietly aside. And the best the cabinet could do on September 12th was to discuss the importance of 'neither applying the brake nor the accelerator to France'.[25]

But Chamberlain's ingenuity was not exhausted. Stimulated anew by Hitler's venomed speech at the Nuremburg party congress (September 12th), a fresh outbreak of disorders (hardly spontaneous) in the Sudetenland, and a pitiable appeal from Paris (September 13th) to find some way to keep Hitler from invading Czechoslovakia and thus invoking the French alliance, he set in motion a plan 'so unconventional and daring that it rather took Halifax's breath away': he offered to go at once to Germany to talk with Hitler.[26] The cabinet approved, after the

[23] Viscount Templewood (Sir Samuel Hoare), *Nine Troubled Years* (London, 1954), p. 298.

[24] The term of Geoffrey Dawson, editor of *The Times* and writer of the leader. Dawson was a close friend of Chamberlain and appeasement.

[25] Colvin, *The Chamberlain Cabinet*, p. 151.

[26] Feiling, *Chamberlain*, p. 357. The idea had emerged several weeks before, but he had saved it as a last expedient. The dramatic quality of his action at the final moment was carefully calculated.

decision was taken, and Hitler cooperated by extending an invitation to Berchtesgaden. Thus began the dramatic trilogy—three visits by Chamberlain to Germany in the space of two weeks—which has come historically to symbolize appeasement.

The pursuit of appeasement into Hitler's lair was risky business, and Chamberlain claimed to know this, though the complexities which might arise from the seemingly simple action were neither carefully nor openly scrutinized. It sealed Britain's direct involvement in the Czechoslovak crisis, identified her with the necessity of a solution, and focused on her the issue of war or peace. But it was also a logical extension of the policy toward Czechoslovakia adopted the previous March, and the risks were nothing, as Chamberlain saw it, when compared to the obvious alternative of war.

At the Berchtesgaden meeting of September 15th, staged in a proper but strained atmosphere at his Alpine retreat, Hitler insisted upon the transfer of the Sudetenland to Germany. Personally prepared to accept this solution, if acceptable procedures were followed, Chamberlain could not commit his government. He proposed, therefore, to return to London for consultation, then visit Hitler again. Impatiently, Hitler consented. The larger and vital question of improving Anglo-German relations as a prelude to the general pacification of Europe was not discussed. Chamberlain tried to raise it, but Hitler cut him off; that must wait until the Czechoslovak issue was settled.[27]

In London again, Chamberlain consulted the inner cabinet,[28] the full cabinet, and the chief French ministers, who flew over from Paris on September 18th. His own commitment to the Sudeten transfer encountered some serious reservations in the cabinet and a vague reluctance on the part of the French. Both were subdued, however, by their inability to counter effectively Chamberlain's conviction that the only alternative was war, and that there was no sense in fighting for a cause which would have to be settled, in any event, in much the same way as he suggested settling it now. There resulted the so-called Anglo-French plan, providing for the cession to Germany of all areas in Czechoslovakia containing more than fifty per cent Germans, and some form of guarantee for the new Czech state, the latter a concession won by the French and conceded by Chamberlain without prior cabinet consultation.[29] As for the Czechs, their initial refusal to accept the plan was shattered by Anglo-French warnings that non-compliance would leave

[27] Chamberlain's report to the cabinet emphasized his opinion that Hitler's objectives were limited and, if Sudeten self-determination were accepted, 'Hitler would not prove too difficult.' Colvin, *The Chamberlain Cabinet*, p. 156.

[28] An unofficial group, comprising Chamberlain, Halifax, Hoare, and Simon (the latter two both ex-foreign secretaries), and official advisers Wilson and Cadogan, which had emerged in impromptu fashion the week before, continued to meet regularly and often in the weeks which followed, and assumed much responsibility for policy-making.

[29] Chamberlain was aware of potential difficulties in implementing a guarantee but he thought its main value would be in its deterrent effect.

them to face their fate alone. So things were ready for Chamberlain to visit Hitler again.

The prearranged second meeting was held in scenic Godesberg on the Rhine, September 22nd–23rd. Bearing concessions which seemed to meet Hitler's basic requirements, Chamberlain was stunned to encounter an obstinate, obstreperous Führer now demanding the immediate German military occupation of the Sudetenland. There followed thirty-six hours of tense, intermittent sparring in which Chamberlain protested the new conditions as constituting an ultimatum and emphasized the impossibility of his agreeing to any plan unless it could be everywhere considered 'as carrying out the principle already agreed upon in an orderly fashion, and free from threat of force'.[30] The result was a modest improvement in Hitler's manners, but not in his demands, though he did offer grudgingly to modify his timetable for military occupation by a few days, while grumbling to Chamberlain that he was the first man to whom he had ever made a concession. At this apparent impasse, Chamberlain returned to London.

The days which followed witnessed a soul-searching seldom paralleled in intensity or strain. Though stung by Hitler's behaviour and senseless demands, Chamberlain was still not convinced that the issue was worth a war. His mind remained fixed on the belief that a peaceful resolution of the Czechoslovak issue, however distasteful, would mark a significant turning point in Anglo-German relations. He was, in short, prepared to accede to Hitler's demands. But opposition to capitulation had begun to stir in the cabinet, especially among some junior ministers, while Chamberlain was still in Godesberg. It appeared in the insistent demand for immediate mobilization by Duff Cooper (first lord of the admiralty) and Hore-Belisha (secretary of state for war) on September 24th. It reached its apex in Halifax's blunt and startling rejection of Hitler's terms the following day, after a crisis of conscience and a complete change of position, apparently influenced by Alexander Cadogan, permanent under-secretary in the foreign office. It was solidified by French concurrence in rejection, during a Daladier-Bonnet visit to London, September 25th, unconditional Czech rejection, and a distinct hardening of feeling against concession in the press and among the British people generally, according to mass-observation surveys.[31]

The way in which Chamberlain and Sir John Simon, the chancellor of the exchequer, tried to manipulate the French into a confession of military hopelessness[32] reveals their continuing conviction that there was no alternative to accepting Hitler's demands. But cabinet objection, embodying the first challenge since Eden's resignation to the prime minister's exclusive control and the policy of appeasement, could not

---

[30] *Documents on British Foreign Policy, 1919–1939*, third series II, pp. 482–3.
[31] The course of cabinet deliberation is detailed in Middlemas, *Diplomacy of Illusion*, pp. 370ff.
[32] See *Documents on British Foreign Policy*, third series II, pp. 520–35.

be casually overridden. So Chamberlain sought, and found, a middle ground: he would send a special emissary, Sir Horace Wilson, to Hitler to urge the formation of an international body of Czechs, Germans, and British to work out the details of the transfer of Sudeten territory. This would keep the door of negotiation open. If Hitler refused, he would be told that France would fight for Czechoslovakia and Britain would stand by France. That should satisfy the critics. A last desperate effort to find a solution short of war, this was also a coolly calculated move, characteristic of the Chamberlain touch in diplomacy.

While Wilson went in search of Hitler, Chamberlain emphasized that, with the quarrel in Czechoslovakia already settled in principle, it must surely be possible to arrange the transfer of territory in a way acceptable to all. Broadcasting to the nation on the night of September 27th, he asserted his readiness 'to pay even a third visit to Germany', while lamenting the 'horrible, fantastic, incredible' fact that Britain was preparing for war 'because of a quarrel in a far-away country between people of whom we know nothing.'[33] In a brusque exchange of messages between Hitler and Chamberlain, via Wilson, the Führer appeared slightly more conciliatory and the prime minister expressed certainty that Hitler could get 'all essentials' without war and without delay. To arrange the settlement, Chamberlain proposed an immediate Anglo-German conference with representatives of Czechoslovakia, and also France and Italy if Hitler so desired.[34] The upshot was Hitler's invitation to Munich which, coming at a time of utmost tension and anxiety, touched off a spectacle of emotional relief in both parliament and the nation at large. Riding on air, both literally and figuratively, Chamberlain departed once more for Germany.[35]

The fact of Munich meant that Hitler had won his essential demands. The Munich agreement,[36] signed by the four heads of state (but not the Czechs, who were not permitted to participate in the deliberations) at 2 a.m. on September 30th, embodied the basic terms of settlement

---

[33] Neville Chamberlain, *In Search of Peace* (New York, 1939), pp. 174–5.

[34] Mussolini's support for this proposal was immediately solicited, and received—a fact sometimes cited as one positive outcome of the Anglo-Italian conversations of March–April 1938.

[35] Hitler's agreement to the conference at Munich forced a last-minute postponement of his scheduled military attack on Czechoslovakia which, since the end of May, had been set for October 1st. It also foiled a scheme, of uncertain dimensions and strength, on the part of an anti-Hitler group in Germany to attempt to remove him from power.

[36] Czech evacuation and German military occupation of the Sudetenland was spread over four zones and seven days. An international commission of German, British, French, Italian, and Czech representatives was assigned the tasks of defining the conditions of evacuation, determining additional territories of predominantly German population to be occupied by October 10th, ascertaining territories in which plebiscites should be held and fixing the conditions of the plebiscites, and finally delimiting the frontier. A German–Czech commission would handle the right of option into and out of transferred territories. The four major powers would guarantee the new frontiers of Czechoslovakia, German and Italian participation hinging on a settlement of Polish and Hungarian minority questions in Czechoslovakia.

prepared by German officials and submitted by Mussolini as their agent. All that Chamberlain could do was attempt to win some modification of the most offensive conditions introduced at Godesberg. Whether he succeeded to any degree at once became, and has since remained, a matter of much debate. But there was no question in Chamberlain's mind. Having long accepted the principle of cession, what he sought at Munich was an orderly, non-violent way for carrying it out. Taken at face value, the terms of Munich seemed to provide that way, and the distressing speed with which it became apparent that those terms could not be so taken had no effect on Chamberlain's assessment.

The prime minister's mind was still alert to the larger issue of Anglo-German relations. Before leaving Munich, and acting entirely alone, he sought out Hitler at his apartment and obtained his signature on a short declaration, of Chamberlain's drafting, which expressed the determination of the two statesmen to continue efforts to remove sources of difference and their intention to employ consultation in dealing with future issues of concern to both countries. Whatever his motives,[37] Chamberlain seemed to believe that he had accomplished something of importance. It was the slip of paper bearing this declaration that he waved in the air, upon his return to London, while making the unfortunate, and apparently unpremeditated, reference to 'peace in our time'.

When men are snatched from the brink of disaster, they are not at once inclined to inquire about the price or who has paid it. So it was in Britain immediately after Munich. The surge of emotion which corresponded with Chamberlain's return as a conquering hero momentarily engulfed nearly all of those who earlier had counselled resistance to Hitler's demands. Within the cabinet, only Duff Cooper registered his protest by resigning. But an intense and dramatic debate in the House of Commons (October 3rd–6th) helped to restore a sense of balance to the nation and encouraged some serious thinking about the broader implications of what had occurred at Munich. There rose from various quarters a crescendo of concern for the future, along with criticism condemning Munich as surrender to force and chastizing the government for betraying the Czechs, killing the League, and estranging Russia. Beneath it all ran the basic imputation that appeasement had failed and must now be replaced by a vigorous, collective approach to security, accompanied by urgent acceleration in rearmament.[38]

But Chamberlain was not impressed by this, and he seemed to have

[37] Estimates of these include the hope of 'cornering' Hitler by binding him to a public declaration and then proclaiming trust in his word; the desire to arrange a situation which, if Hitler broke his word, would convince America of his dishonesty; the need for some larger gain to justify to his countrymen the sacrifice of Czecho-slovakia; the belief in Hitler's sincerity and the hope of advancing the general cause of appeasement.

[38] See Rock, *Appeasement on Trial*, pp. 139–61.

undiminished support, in numbers, if not in degree of confidence, in cabinet and Commons. Prepared to concede that appeasement could not be quickly and easily attained, and that Britain must work to reduce her armament deficiencies, he nevertheless believed that, with the Czechoslovak problem out of the way, it was possible to make further progress 'along the road to sanity', including perhaps an agreement with the dictators to stop the armaments race. Thus the experiences of September, however much they shook the faith of others in the efficacy of appeasement, confirmed for Chamberlain and his closest colleagues the need for further pursuit of the policy. In consequence, the months which followed Munich, tranquil on the surface but anxious underneath, constitute the 'golden age' of appeasement.

Determined to keep things 'on the move', as he wrote to his sister after a short vacation in Scotland, Chamberlain proposed to the Commons in early November 'a further step forward in the policy of appeasement'—implementation of the Anglo-Italian agreement of April. The announced withdrawal of ten thousand Italian infantrymen from Spain, assurances from Mussolini about the future removal of all who remained, and consequently the elimination of the Spanish question as a menace to the peace of Europe were, he said, the bases for his action. This provoked bitter charges of surrender, betrayal, and naive credulity from parliamentary critics (Labourites, Liberals and dissident Conservatives), who questioned the extent to which previously stated British conditions prerequisite to enforcement had been satisfied. Chamberlain's interpretation of fulfilment was indeed a generous one, but his wish prevailed by a large majority of 200 votes.

The effort to improve relations with Italy, which Chamberlain now regarded as essential to any détente with Germany, required the soothing of irritations in Franco-Italian relations. To promote that end, and for other reasons,[39] Chamberlain sought an invitation to Paris and journeyed there with Halifax on November 24th. A 'complete identity of ideas' on a wide range of policy issues was attained only by grudging French acquiescence to British pressure on one crucial point: the international guarantee to rump Czechoslovakia was not to be interpreted as a fixed moral obligation but a flexible possibility contingent upon Italo-German attitudes and the future course of events.[40] The official record does not reveal that Chamberlain mentioned his intention to visit Rome (Mussolini had invited him to do so at Munich), which was very much in his mind at the time.

The post-Munich shift of emphasis in appeasement from Germany to Italy was no doubt influenced by disturbing evidence that Germany

[39] Chamberlain's own explanation included giving the French people an opportunity to express their gratitude to him, encouraging Daladier to make stronger efforts in defence and national unity, and assuring France that Britain would not forget old allies. Feiling, *Chamberlain*, p. 389.
[40] See *Documents on British Foreign Policy*, third series III, pp. 285–311, for a record of the conversation.

was simply not interested in a broad agreement with Britain and was, in fact, plainly contemptuous of Britain's strength, vitality, and consequent importance.[41] Chamberlain said as much in the cabinet on November 30th; acknowledging that prospects for appeasement were not bright in Berlin, he thought it might be useful for him to visit Rome. He elaborated in the cabinet of December 21st, noting his 'definite purpose of securing Signor Mussolini's good offices in Berlin'. Hopefully, Mussolini could, and would, discourage Hitler from undertaking 'some mad dog act'.[42]

By nearly all accounts save his own, Chamberlain's visit to Rome with Halifax on January 11th–13th accomplished nothing. There was no agenda and the rambling talk about Anglo-Italian relations was drab and indecisive. Efforts to engage Mussolini in confidential discussion of Hitler and his future intentions got nowhere. At first that disappointed Chamberlain, but he then decided, as he told the cabinet on January 18th, that it reflected credit on Mussolini's character. The Duce's decision to skip the farewell banquet in favour of a skiing party suggests the importance he attached to it all. But Chamberlain was satisfied, and convinced that his visit had strengthened the cause of peace. He had found Mussolini frank and considerate (others in the British party thought him curt and discourteous), and emphatic in his desire for peace. And the prime minister was much impressed by the exuberant greeting accorded him by the Italian people, to which he attached considerable importance.

Meanwhile, evidence was accumulating to suggest that appeasement was further than ever from realization, and quite possibly beyond it. Hitler's intense dissatisfaction with Munich, which gradually leaked back to the cabinet, was reflected in his brutal treatment of Czechoslovakia and its steady slide under German domination. A savage antisemitic pogrom in Germany in mid-November left the British aghast at such barbarity. The Führer's sarcastic references in public speeches to British 'governesses' and 'umbrella-carrying types', and the venomous attacks on Britain in the German press, forced Chamberlain to admit his disappointment with the German attitude, and even to allow that Britain might be dealing with a man whose actions were not rational. A report in mid-December of German plans for a surprise air attack on London—which the cabinet took seriously enough to post an anti-aircraft regiment in Wellington barracks, within easy view of the German embassy—was hardly reassuring; nor was a scare in January occasioned by reports, subsequently proved false, of an impending German attack on Holland. Italy's attitude was not much better, Mussolini regularly ridiculing the degenerate democracies and

---

[41] Such evidence was summarized by Halifax in the foreign policy committee of the cabinet, November 14th (see Middlemas, *Diplomacy of Illusion*, pp. 432–3), and noted in the cabinet on other occasions during the winter of 1938–39.

[42] Colvin, *The Chamberlain Cabinet*, p. 176.

rigging an outcry for 'Nice, Tunis, Corsica!' in the Italian Chamber of Deputies.

All this was accompanied by intensifying scepticism about appeasement in sections of the British parliament and press, and stinging reversals for supporters of Chamberlain in scattered by-elections. Even British banking was adversely affected, for many foreign depositors closed their accounts in the apparent belief, as Simon told the cabinet on January 18th, that war was coming and Britain might not be ready for it. But these unpalatable factors had little observable effect on the Chamberlain attitude toward policy, save for quickening impatience with those who questioned it,[43] and strengthening efforts to establish confidence by talking it into being. Moments of discouragement seemed to spark a determination that doubt must be forbidden. Appeasement was still the right, the only, policy for the nation, and it must be followed through to success.

Trusting unduly in a variety of deterrent forces which he believed would help to restrain Hitler,[44] Chamberlain also drew encouragement from several other factors. If the political appeasement of Germany was momentarily side-tracked after Munich, efforts to improve Anglo-German economic relations moved ahead with some success.[45] With Chamberlain, Halifax, and Simon prepared to concede German economic predominance in central and southeastern Europe, improved economic relations seemed likely, and this, it was hoped, would have a favourable effect on political relations. In addition, British rearmament was thought to be making important advances. Here the emphasis was still essentially on defensive preparations (fighter aircraft, air-raid precautions and anti-aircraft defence), planning far outdistanced actual production, and many measures were calculated more on the need to soothe an alarmed public opinion and to bolster French morale than to provide coherent policy that would enable the nation to face a critical situation. Nevertheless, the prime minister wrote in February that Hitler had 'missed the bus' at Munich; 'they could not make nearly such a mess of us now as they could have done then, while we could make much more of a mess of them.'[46] And speaking at Blackburn on February

[43] L. B. Namier sagaciously observed about Munich: 'The more there was of doubt lurking deeper down, the greater was at first the annoyance and irritation with anyone who dared to give expression to it.' 'Munich Survey: A Summing Up', *Listener* XL (December 2nd, 1948), p. 836.

[44] Among them were the peaceful sentiments of the German and Italian people, Mussolini's influence with Hitler, talk of impending economic crisis in Germany, and Poland's second thoughts about its non-aggression pact of 1934 with Germany. See Iain Macleod, *Neville Chamberlain* (London, 1961), p. 272.

[45] Conversations between representatives of the coal industry resulted in agreement (January) to divide coal export markets. Proposals exchanged by the British Federation of Industries and the Reich Federation of Industry culminated in planning for a joint meeting in Düsseldorf in mid-March, about the same time as Oliver Stanley, president of the board of trade, was scheduled to visit Berlin.

[46] Feiling, *Chamberlain*, p. 394; Macleod, *Chamberlain*, p. 272.

22nd, he quoted Shakespeare: 'Come the three corners of the world in arms, and we shall shock them.'[47]

There resulted a kind of ministerial euphoria, partly contrived and partly real. Against the judgement of Halifax and the foreign office, and in defiance of troublesome signs in Czechoslovakia, Chamberlain and a few other ministers, notably Simon and Hoare, seemed to compete in issuing optimistic statements to the nation. The climax came in Hoare's address in Chelsea (March 10th) which, at Chamberlain's urging, referred to the possible imminence of a 'golden age'. The same day Chamberlain assured assembled press correspondents that Europe was settling down to a period of tranquility.

They could not have been more mistaken. The brutal German conquest of rump Czechoslovakia, which shockingly exceeded Hitler's long professed objective of taking only Germans into the Reich, occurred just five days later (March 15th). Stunned and dismayed, Chamberlain's first reaction was to treat the event lightly. Explaining to the House of Commons that Czechoslovakia had disintegrated because of 'internal disruption'—which freed the British government from any obligation to her—he conceded violation of the spirit of Munich but not the discrediting of appeasement and implored the members:

> Do not let us on that account be deflected from our course. Let us remember that the desire of all peoples of the world still remains concentrated on the hopes of peace. . . Though we may have to suffer checks and disappointments from time to time, the object that we have in mind is of too great significance to the happiness of mankind for us lightly to give it up or set it on one side.[48]

But the language of appeasement was that day alien in the House of Commons. It provoked fierce criticism and induced a pitch of anger rarely seen. Many government supporters shared the deep dissatisfaction of former critics with the inadequacy of Chamberlain's response, and Simon's efforts to rally support by warning against extensive and un-defined commitments only exacerbated a deteriorating situation. This radical change of temper also appeared at once in all sections of the British press,[49] which seemed to reflect an explosion of public discontent across the nation. Nearly everywhere, the reduction of Munich to utter mockery was seen as totally discrediting appeasement and finally compelling its abandonment.

Chamberlain was not easily moved, however. March 16th revealed no apparent change in his outlook; his replies to questions about Czechoslovakia in the Commons were vague and noncommital. But

---

[47] *German White Book: Documents on the Events Preceding the Outbreak of War* (New York, 1940), p. 269.
[48] *House of Commons Debates*, March 15th, 1939, col. 435–40.
[49] See Rock, *Appeasement on Trial*, pp. 207–9.

on March 17th the accumulating pressure from parliament, press, Conservative party (where insurrection was brewing), foreign office, cabinet, and service chiefs had its effect. Scheduled to speak in Birmingham, the prime minister cast aside a text on domestic issues and grasped the international nettle. He did not expound a new policy or commission a new crusade, but he showed himself aware of the dangerous implications in Germany's action, raised some crucial questions about the future, and declared his readiness to resist domination of the world by force. Next day he told the cabinet of his new conviction that Hitler's attitude 'made it impossible to continue to negotiate on the old basis with the Nazi regime.'[50]

Impelled by the force of events and an insistent parliamentary and popular demand for new and different initiatives, two weeks of frantic diplomatic activity followed. In view of a reported German economic ultimatum to Rumania, the British sought 'expressions of opinion' from Paris, Moscow, Warsaw, Ankara, Athens, and Belgrade. Russia proposed an immediate conference, possibly in Bucharest, to discuss the possibility of common action. Britain rejected that with some unconvincing arguments[51] in favour of a 'bold and startling' (Chamberlain's words) scheme to associate France, Russia, and Poland with her in a declaration that, in the event of a threat to the independence of any European nation, the four powers would consult at once on measures for common resistance. This proposal foundered on Poland's refusal to be so associated with the Soviet Union. Confronted with a choice between Russia and Poland, the British decided on Poland, considered the more formidable military ally. In fact, Chamberlain and Halifax, in consultation with Bonnet, apparently decided and the cabinet accepted the decision.[52] The unilateral guarantee of Polish independence issued on March 31st was an improvisation which emerged when the intense and unrelenting pressure on Chamberlain to 'do something' to meet the German danger was suddenly reinforced by a swift accumulation of reports that Poland was the next object of German aggression, and imminently so.[53]

The guarantee to Poland (and similar guarantees extended on April 13th to Rumania and Greece, following the Italian invasion of Albania) was widely regarded as constituting a genuine revolution in British foreign policy—and rightly so insofar as the acceptance of continental commitments was concerned. Chamberlain called it 'a portent . . .

[50] Colvin, *The Chamberlain Cabinet*, p. 188.
[51] These included the difficulty of sending a responsible minister to participate and the danger of holding a conference without the certainty of success. *Documents on British Foreign Policy*, third series IV, pp. 392–3.
[52] Colvin, *The Chamberlain Cabinet*, pp. 191–3.
[53] On the circumstances of the issuance of the guarantee to Poland, see William R. Rock, 'The British Guarantee to Poland, March, 1939: a Problem in Diplomatic Decision-making', *South Atlantic Quarterly* LXV, no. 2 (1966), pp. 229–40. See also Keith Eubank, 'The British Pledge to Poland: Prelude to War', *Southwestern Social Science Quarterly* XLV, no. 4 (1965), pp. 340–48.

so momentous that . . . it will have a chapter to itself when the history books come to be written.'[54] Marking as it did a rude and final awakening to the Nazi menace, and signalling the opening of efforts, however halting, to construct a peace front in Europe against further fascist aggression, it might also have heralded the final abandonment of appeasement. But there is little to show that such an effect was intended. Chamberlain did not regard war as inevitable and was still 'unwilling to believe' that his efforts to remove suspicion and promote peace and goodwill would not 'even yet bear fruit'.[55] Thus the diplomacy of the next five months was aimed as much, or more, at restraining Hitler and inclining him at length toward the conference table as at forming an impressive phalanx against Germany or advancing preparations for impending war. 'There was still a hope', as A. J. P. Taylor aptly puts it, 'of conciliating Hitler under the determination to resist him, just as previously there had been an inclination to resist under the top layer of appeasement'.[56] But it required more propitious circumstances and these never arose.

With active appeasement side-tracked, appeasement attitudes still affected decisions both in domestic and foreign affairs. The enacting of conscription in late April, pressed on Chamberlain against his will and approved primarily to hearten the French and pacify British opinion, was carefully accompanied by Nevile Henderson's return to Berlin (he had been recalled after March 15th) to explain the British action before it was announced in the Commons. When Chamberlain at length agreed, under heavy pressure, to establish a ministry of supply, he avoided naming Churchill (widely regarded as the obvious man for the job) to head it; he did not want to jeopardize 'any possibility of easing the tension and getting back to normal relations with the dictators' by making an appointment that 'would certainly be regarded as a challenge'.[57] Similar considerations figured prominently in the prime minister's refusal of cabinet reconstruction.

This outlook surely affected the Anglo-French negotiations with Russia which aimed at her inclusion in a European peace front. These began in mid-April and, amid a tide of popular interest and impatience, dragged into mid-August, when they were abruptly terminated by a development the British had thought impossible—Russia's signing of a non-aggression pact with Germany.[58] Beginning the talks 'in order to placate our left wing in England, rather than to obtain any solid

---

[54] *House of Commons Debates*, April 3rd, 1939, col. 2481ff.
[55] *ibid.*, April 13th, 1939, col. 15.
[56] A. J. P. Taylor, *The Origins of the Second World War* (London, 1961), p. 204.
[57] Feiling, *Chamberlain*, p. 406.
[58] These negotiations have been described in a number of works. See in particular, A. J. P. Taylor, *Englishman and Others* (London, 1956), pp. 157–67; and William R. Rock, 'Grand Alliance or Daisy Chain: British Opinion and Policy Toward Russia, April–August, 1939', in Lillian P. Wallace and William Askew (editors), *Power, Public Opinion, and Diplomacy* (Durham, 1959), pp. 297–337.

military advantage',[59] and pursuing them with great caution and deliberation because 'we are not preparing for war, we are constructing a peace front',[60] the British had sought an agreement which would provide for Russian aid in eastern Europe if and when it was needed. But they never grasped the Russians' sense of urgency and fear for their own security, and consequently never moved sufficiently to satisfy Russia's stern and escalating (given her superior bargaining position) requirements for a pact of mutual aid. Rather, wary of Russia's intentions— 'getting everyone else by the ears', as Chamberlain put it—and sceptical of her military value, the British were more intent on keeping the Soviet Union out of eastern Europe and the Baltic states than on obtaining her assistance against future German aggression.

As the summer of 1939 wore on and an ominous German campaign against Poland intensified, there were only a few instances of note in which the dying policy of appeasement appeared. These related to what have been described as 'energetic efforts to see if Germany's general economic and colonial aspirations could be met without vital sacrifices of interest on the part of the western powers',[61] and British hesitation attending Germany's campaign against Poland. The former is symbolized by the visit of Helmut Wohltat, a major German economic official, to London during the third week of July. Conversations with Horace Wilson and R. S. Hudson, minister of overseas trade, suggest a British hope to defuse the Polish issue by eclipsing it with an Anglo-German agreement on broader issues—economic cooperation, including a delimitation of spheres of influence and a possible loan to Germany, colonial questions, a limitation of armaments, possibly even a non-aggression pact. But there was no follow-up from Berlin, and the episode is notable mainly for what it reveals about the persistence of British hopes for reconciliation with Germany.

The shocking news of the Russo-German non-aggression pact (August 23rd) was met by a straightforward reaffirmation of Britain's commitment to Poland, a sentiment which echoed unmistakably throughout the nation. But the last week of peace witnessed frantic British efforts to bring the Germans and Poles together on a negotiated settlement, and to hold open the possibility of a new Anglo-German treaty if only the Germans would act with reason in resolving the Polish question. Cabinet deliberations during those days of tension hinted at a temptation to return once more to the ways of the past and to grasp with eager hands anything Hitler might have to offer. But Hitler showed no interest in a freely negotiated settlement with Poland, and the mood of the British nation, parliament in particular, precluded acceptance of anything less. A return to appeasement was out of the question.

---

[59] The words of Alexander Cadogan, permanent under-secretary in the foreign office, in a cabinet minute, April 19th. Colvin, *The Chamberlain Cabinet*, p. 200.

[60] The words of Sir John Simon in the cabinet committee on foreign policy, June 5th. *ibid.*, p. 216.

[61] Northedge, *The Troubled Giant*, p. 606.

The German attack on Poland on September 1st was followed by two days of British temporizing in honouring her guarantee, and the declaration of war on Germany on September 3rd was forced by near revolt in the House of Commons and a threatened strike by a number of ministers. Official explanations for delay centred mainly on French reluctance to act until her mobilization and initial defence preparations were well advanced, and the need to coordinate Anglo-French action. But Chamberlain's stated willingness to negotiate with Germany if the invasion were halted and German troops withdrawn, and his hope that Germany might yet agree to an Italian proposal for an international conference on terms which Britain could accept, demonstrate his nearly indestructible attachment to the idea of a negotiated settlement with Germany which might yet bring European stability. After the outbreak of war, he remained optimistic that it could be won without a major decision in the field, a view not generally shared by his colleagues. But such a victory could result only from internal German developments, not from a further effort at appeasement. That policy lay dead and discredited.

2 The Meaning and Nature of Appeasement

As D. C. Watt pointed out a decade ago, the term appeasement has passed irretrievably into historical usage to describe the period of European diplomacy preceding the outbreak of the Second World War. It has become fossilized in history and has acquired the 'status of a myth—loaded with implication, undertones and overtones'[1], to such a degree that one is tempted by W. N. Medlicott's suggestion that appeasement be added to imperialism on the list of terms no scholar uses. But instead of this, it is well to consider briefly the nature and meaning of the term in its historical context.

Appeasement is an emotive term, imprecise and ambiguous. Any attempt at definition meets with problems of semantics, to say nothing of value theory, political philosophy, and empirical judgement. This has been especially so in recent years; it was also true of the period 1937–39, when Chamberlain was actively pursuing the policy. Indeed, few efforts at genuine definition were undertaken during the policy's implementation as a calculated technique of British foreign policy in the latter 1930s. In consequence, the term took on divergent meanings in the minds of supporters and critics, who came to assume the validity and general acceptance of their conception of policy and to demonstrate increasing irritation with those who did not conform to their view of things. For many Englishmen, no clear-cut definition ever did emerge, with the result that there was always a mass of opinion which stood somewhere between the poles of support and dissent, sometimes accepting, consciously or unconsciously, portions of this or that meaning and open more perhaps to the influence of feeling than cool political reasoning.

This much is clear: in the realm of semantics, appeasement gradually changed during the latter 1930s from a 'good' or neutral term, used by a rather wide range of British policy-makers and accepted as respectable in the currency of political discussion, into a word or concept with a 'bad' connotation. Its ultimate failure to achieve its primary objective, the conciliation of Nazi Germany, and its consequent contribution to the outbreak of war—the degree of 'responsibility' remains a matter of lively dispute among historians—so discredited the policy that meanings

[1] D. C. Watt, 'Appeasement: the Rise of a Revisionist School?', *The Political Quarterly* XXXVI, no. 2 (1965), p. 191.

ascribed to it since the traumatic 1930s embody a definite degeneration in the concept as it emerged in Britain earlier. Currently, appeasement has become so vague, ambiguous, and all-inclusive as to embrace almost any policy one wants to brand as weak, vacillating, or indeterminate. But this was not the case in Britain in the 1930s.

The transformation is graphically demonstrated by standard dictionary entries which before the Second World War defined appeasement in terms of pacification (soothing, quieting, or calming) in the genuine sense, aiming in international politics at the reduction of tension and the promotion of harmony. Post-war editions began to add a second dimension: the concept of conciliation by means of buying-off, usually involving a sacrifice of principle in order to avert aggression, and examples making specific reference to Munich began to appear. More recently, appeasement as 'a policy of appeasing a potential aggressor', without specific reference to method but with a clearly negative connotation, is distinguished from pacification in a general sense, and it is in the former sense that the term is most frequently used.

The treatment of appeasement by an eminent American scholar of international politics, Hans J. Morgenthau, further illustrates this point. Appeasement is described as:

> a foreign policy that attempts to meet the threat of imperialism with methods appropriate to a policy of the status quo. . . . It errs in transferring a policy of compromise from a political environment favourable to the preservation of the status quo, where it belongs, to an environment exposed to imperialistic attack, where it does not belong. One might say that appeasement is a corrupted policy of compromise, made erroneous by mistaking a policy of imperialism for a policy of the status quo.[2]

The terms 'errs', 'corrupted policy', and 'made erroneous' signify the invalidity of appeasement according to this definition. And the point is clinched a few paragraphs later: 'Appeasement, which is the attempt to compromise with an imperialism not recognized as such, and the fear that creates imperialism where there is none—these are the two wrong answers, the two fatal mistakes an intelligent foreign policy must try to avoid.'[3] However acceptable to contemporary political scientists and scholars of international affairs, this analysis of appeasement derives largely from the historical experience of the 1930s; it does not reflect a view generally held by Englishmen, or others, in 1937.

Degeneration in the concept of appeasement appeared during 1937–38, as Chamberlain's efforts failed and disillusionment with the policy grew, especially among those elements earlier inclined to be sceptical. There are substantial grounds for holding, as Martin Gilbert

[2] Hans J. Morgenthau, *Politics among Nations: The Struggle for Power and Peace* (New York, 1967), p. 61.
[3] *ibid.*, pp. 65–6.

does, that Munich, commonly cited as the epitome of appeasement, was a very different phenomenon from appeasement in its earlier context.[4] Whereas appeasement was a traditional policy based upon concessions made from a position of strength, within limits always controllable by the appeaser, Munich involved emergency compliance with the demands of the adversary in an atmosphere of desperation, and, some would say, from a position of weakness. It brought peace at the price of the disintegration of Czechoslovakia (not a party to the negotiations) and the transfer of non-Nazis to Nazi rule without a plebiscite. Further,

> Appeasement's justification, whether at the time of the American Revolution or of the Lausanne conference on reparations, was that it was rooted in a deep concern for considerations of international morality, and that however expedient specific acts of appeasement might be, they were also moral. 'Munich' may have been expedient, but it had less of an aura of morality.[5]

It is unlikely that Munich will ever be dissociated from appeasement generally in the popular mind; it has stood too long as the symbolic term for the policy, and distinctions like that above are easily dismissed as slyly academic. Yet the distinction is vital in assessing the roles of those who at least tolerated, if they did not encourage and support, Chamberlain's early initiatives at appeasement, but found the Munich agreement impossible to accept.

Another kind of distinction must also be made, between passive and active appeasement.[6] The former involves the impromptu and piecemeal sanctioning of an adversary's advance—by means of armament amassing treaty violation, or the development of economic and ideological spheres of interest—to a more powerful position in an area where the appeasing power has vital interests; mere failure to respond in any way is not appeasement. The latter begins with a sympathetic hearing for the concrete grievances and demands laid down by a potentially or actively aggressive adversary, perhaps even with an invitation to formulate and state grievances or demands more clearly, and proceeds through negotiation towards the satisfaction of the demands. Both may be, but are not necessarily, accompanied by moral considerations. The passive approach, pragmatic and unplanned, was largely characteristic of Stanley Baldwin's foreign policy with respect to Europe; Chamberlain initiated the phase of active appeasement, a new era of efforts aimed directly at confronting and resolving certain major

---

[4] Martin Gilbert, *The Roots of Appeasement* (London, 1966), pp. 179ff.

[5] *ibid.*, p. 179. The 'immorality' of the appeasers of the thirties derived especially from their readiness 'to put the freedom from fascist control of individuals, groups, and entire nations on the bargaining counter; or ultimately, even to make it a matter of unilateral concession'. John H. Herz, 'The Relevancy and Irrelevancy of Appeasement', *Social Research* xxxi, no. 3 (1964), p. 318.

[6] See George A. Lanyi, 'The Problem of Appeasement', *World Politics* xv, no. 2 (1963), p. 319.

problems that were poisoning the life of Europe. Evaluations of these respective phases of appeasement vary, especially in relation to the changing situations in those nations which were the object of appeasement. But there is little doubt that one not only preceded, but in some respects conditioned, the other—a fact of considerable importance in any assessment of total responsibility for British appeasement. It is also true, however, that Chamberlain's brand of appeasement marked a more radical departure from earlier tradition than has usually been described by historians, and that there is no reason to suppose that it was inevitable or without alternative.[7]

All this says something about the broader dimensions of appeasement, but it still leaves the term, as used in reference to British policy in the latter 1930s, considerably short of clarity. That is best sought by examining what the policy meant to Chamberlain and his colleagues. The keynote here is simplicity, for while a wide array of motive forces clearly conditioned their thinking (see chapter 4), their initial, basic understanding of what it was that needed to be done, and how it should be undertaken, was certainly not complex.[8]

Confronted by an increasingly tense and potentially combustible Europe, produced in particular by the rising tempo of aggressive attitudes and actions on the part of Fascist Italy and Nazi Germany, who claimed unremitted grievances left from the First World War and Versailles, Chamberlain proposed to bring these nations into friendly discussion with Britain and France in order to 'arrive at what has sometimes been called a general settlement, to arrive at a position . . . when reasonable grievances may be removed, when suspicions may be laid aside, and when confidence may again be restored'.[9] He did not intend to ask for firm reciprocal advantages; rather, he sought only the assurance of future 'mutual understanding'. Success in this endeavour, Chamberlain believed, would save the peace of Europe for a generation. But it could not be achieved by sitting still and waiting for something to turn up. Rather, 'you have got to set about it. You have got to inform yourself what are the difficulties . . . and when you have found that out, you must exert yourself to find the remedy.'[10]

Like most of his countrymen, Chamberlain did not approve of the German and Italian dictatorships; he loathed the internal excesses of both, especially the police state aspects of Nazism. But since Britain

---

[7] Middlemas, *Diplomacy of Illusion*, pp. 2, 43.

[8] Gilbert and Gott, *The Appeasers*, has as its major purpose 'to show what the appeasers sought and what methods they were prepared to use in order to attain their ends'. (Foreword).

[9] *House of Commons Debates*, December 21st, 1937, col. 1804–7. Russia was to be excluded. See p. 50.

[10] Speech in Birmingham, April 8th, 1938. Chamberlain, *In Search of Peace*, p. 98. This theme appears over and over in Chamberlain's speeches, both in parliament and elsewhere, nearly always accompanied by reference to the need for rearmament sufficient to ensure that Britain's voice, when raised for peace, would be heard with respect.

could not remove the dictators, she must try to live in peace with them, losing no opportunity to remove those grievances deemed genuine and legitimate. Apart from improving immediate diplomatic relations, this might strengthen pacific elements in Germany and Italy, reduce the internal value of war propaganda, allow the fascist revolutions to become respectable, and open the way to peace for all.

Chamberlain believed the dictators had good reason to ask the remedy of certain grievances in international affairs, and was prepared to go a considerable distance in recognizing the 'legitimate interests' of both. Refusing to consider sacred existing political arrangements such as boundaries and colonial possessions, consequently uncommitted to the maintenance of the status quo, and apparently oblivious to, or contemptuous of, some of the subtler aspects of power balance, he was willing to negotiate change in the interest of peace; his attitude is exemplified by the view that if he could purchase peace and a lasting settlement with Germany by handing over Tanganyika, he would not hesitate for a moment. The only condition he laid down was that changes should take place peacefully, as a result of open negotiation unattended by force or the threat of force. Dealing with the dictators in this way involved a certain risk, of which Chamberlain often declared himself aware. But it was nothing compared to the only alternative he saw— the continued embitterment of feelings 'until at last the barriers are broken down and the conflict begins which many think would mark the end of civilization'.[11] Chamberlain's policy was so reasonable, in his own view, that it was hard to see how anyone could possibly oppose it.

At first only a few did so, but the number steadily increased as time passed and the quickening tempo of German and Italian belligerence persuaded a growing circle of Englishmen that appeasement was failing to attain its objective. As the Czechoslovak crisis of 1938 ran its course, Chamberlain's sharpest critics came to interpret appeasement as sheer surrender to unscrupulous demands, largely from motives of fear or indolence, propelled by a frantic desire to avoid sacrificing anything of value to himself. Not only did this smack of immorality, it also dangerously weakened the appeasers' relative power position and whetted the voracious appetite of the adversary. In their eyes, the policy became so dangerous that it was hard to see how anyone could possibly support it. In consequence, the wisdom of appeasement became a matter of mounting controversy, tinged with deep emotion and intensity of feeling, in English political life.[12] And any former element of consensus about the meaning of the term and policy quickly disappeared.

Beyond the idea of approaching the dictators and negotiating redress of their grievances, there are additional aspects of appeasement which,

---

[11] *House of Commons Debates*, February 21st, 1938, col. 64.
[12] The development of criticism and open opposition to appeasement, from February 1938, to the outbreak of war, is detailed in Rock, *Appeasement on Trial*.

while not essential to the basic concept, became integrally associated with the policy as pursued by Chamberlain and his colleagues. Their policy rested on the assumption that the dictators were reasonable men, open to argument and persuasion. Chamberlain was unwilling to believe that the leaders of other states could have such an utterly different outlook on life from his own as to contemplate war except for purposes of self-defence. 'Human nature, which is the same all the world over, must reject the nightmare [war] with all its might,' he proclaimed at the lord mayor's banquet in the Guildhall on November 9th, 1937. For any government to do otherwise would be to betray the trust of its people and earn the condemnation of all mankind, and he did 'not believe that such a government anywhere exists among civilized peoples'. Thus he was certain that a way could be found 'to free the world from the curse of armaments and the fears that give rise to them and to open up a happier and wiser future for mankind'.[13]

This faith became a dominant element in Chamberlain's thought. He clung to appeasement with amazing, or appalling, tenacity, refusing to modify his estimate of its chances for success or to revise his appraisal of his adversaries, despite the gradual accumulation of cogent evidence, which he sometimes frankly acknowledged, to support another view. Appeasement must succeed because he and the British people wanted it to succeed, he implied on sundry occasions, thus revealing a crucial failure to distinguish wish from prospect. Britain had a special part to play, as conciliator and mediator, in 'making gentle' the life of Europe. Appeasement thus took on the character of a mission. And as the urgency of the mission grew, and commitment to it deepened, the prime minister saw what he wished to see. This made it easier to revise or ignore past judgements on the nature of the dictators and their regimes and to disregard incongruous and disturbing elements as they arose.[14]

Regular reference to Chamberlain, or to the prime minister and a few close colleagues, is not meant to imply that they alone devised appeasement apart from the sentiments of the English people and pursued it stubbornly against the popular will. The influence and eventual isolation of the prime minister and the relatively small group of men clustered around him at the summit of power—a condition which they themselves promoted—make it easy to think in terms of just a few 'appeasers' on whom all responsibility must ultimately come to rest. But the currents of appeasement in Britain in the mid-1930s were exceedingly strong; that Chamberlain initially had the sympathy, and generally the active support, of a vast majority of his countrymen is beyond any doubt. Whether this was grounded in ignorance, indifference, realism, or idealism is of no consequence to the basic matter of fact, though the question deserves greater historical examination and

[13] Chamberlain, *In Search of Peace*, p. 29.
[14] See Christopher Thorne, *The Approach of War, 1938–1939* (London, 1967), pp. 20–21.

analysis than it has yet received. So appeasement was a highly personal policy in terms of the way in which Chamberlain pursued it and the influence he wielded in shaping it; but it was also, in initial conception and continuing temperamental context, a genuine national policy in terms of its broad compatibility with the English frame of mind.[15] This certainly changed over time, but then only involved a different reading of the requirements of political realism, not a fundamental rejection in principle of the aims and objectives of the prime minister. In this regard, appeasement stands as a basically English phenomenon. Certainly, it received the support of many Frenchmen and was widely accepted by default in the United States. But of the many forces behind the policy (see chapter 4), some were uniquely British in origin and 'design'.

The element of method in Chamberlain's pursuit of appeasement also merits attention here, for it came to be widely regarded as a vital part of the policy itself. In Chamberlain's view, a settlement of differences with the dictators could be accomplished only through direct discussion with them. He had learned through many years of experience as a successful Birmingham businessman that the best way to resolve business disputes was through a quiet and orderly process of face-to-face negotiation, culminating at length in mutual compromise and conciliation.[16] Why should the same method not be used for dealing with international problems? Taking at face value Hitler's repeated declarations that his territorial aims were limited to securing application of the principle of self-determination (which, the Führer once reminded him, had not been formulated by Germany), and assuming that Hitler's ambitions were limited to obtaining an overdue measure of justice for Germany, Chamberlain could not believe that disputes arising within these limited fields could not be solved by the sensible, give-and-take methods with which two businessmen would iron out some complication in the dealings between their respective firms.

He was all the more bent on personal action because of his lack of confidence in the foreign office. Suspecting the existence of an irresponsible foreign office mentality, unrelated to the practical realities of Britain's strategic and economic position and bound by tradition, Chamberlain grew impatient both because it did not seem to move quickly or vigorously enough for the crisis threatening Europe and because the contacts which it established through normal channels had a habit of 'running into the sand'. Thus convinced that he should deal directly with those who controlled foreign policy in other nations,

---

[15] Any separation of appeasement from the English temper of the 1930s is as unconvincing as those efforts which have sometimes been made to separate the phenomenon of Nazism from the thought and feeling of the German people generally.

[16] Much has been written about Chamberlain's 'businessman's approach' to foreign relations. The point can be, and has sometimes been, exaggerated, but it is undeniable that his thinking was conditioned by his long years of business experience. See William R. Rock, *Neville Chamberlain* (New York, 1969), pp. 31–3.

he began to employ special emissaries, to maintain contact with the German and Italian ambassadors in London through confidants, and most importantly, to develop at 10 Downing Street what appeared to be his own little foreign office, headed by Sir Horace Wilson, which informed, advised, humoured, and shielded Chamberlain, and generally promulgated his ideas on foreign affairs. Its usurpation of normal foreign office functions caused both resentment in that office and a lack of coordination in the administration of foreign affairs. In his zeal for action, Chamberlain thus initiated a controversial aspect of policy formulation and execution, an aspect so closely associated with appeasement that it came to be widely regarded as an essential component of the policy itself.

In summary, appeasement in the historical context of the latter 1930s was initially a policy of actively identifying the basic grievances of disgruntled powers, particularly Germany and Italy, and attempting to negotiate removal of those grievances through reasonable concessions in the face of legitimate demands, thus opening the way for a general settlement that would ensure the continuation of peace for all. Chamberlain added the method of proceeding via personal contact with chiefs of state. The policy was undertaken not from cowardice or fear, but from a strong sense of mission impelled by a variety of practical considerations and tempered by the combination of guilty conscience and superior morality. In its earlier phases, it embodied the political sentiment of a strong majority of Englishmen. Its failure to attain quickly the desired objectives resulted in efforts to promote its success which, in the minds of a gradually increasing number, went dangerously beyond the original concept of the policy. This raised questions about its limitations and 'workability', prompted a growing body of scepticism and criticism, and opened the way for confusion and controversy over both definition and validity—confusion and controversy which continue in one form or another to the present time and will probably continue as long as the balance of power remains an important element in international politics.

3 The Origins and Early Development of Appeasement

Efforts to identify and measure the influence of a nation's past on its later development are vital and intriguing aspects of historical study. Cause-and-effect relationships, especially as they can be established over a broad period of time, provide an element of continuity, and thus an 'explanatory essence', without which history would appear as a frightful jumble of unrelated experiences. Consequently, major historical episodes are subjected to careful scrutiny with regard to their roots, origins, or antecedents. But the extent to which prior events and influences necessarily precondition and determine the form and nature of the developments of later years remains, in most cases, a matter of interpretation and often lively conjecture among historians. Exaggerated emphasis on cause and effect, or continuity, can result in questionable theories of determinism or inevitability; too little emphasis can produce over-simplistic and unsatisfying explanations of chance or coincidence.

The question of 'how far back' one may trace the origins of appeasement is not easily answered. That Neville Chamberlain added an important element to appeasement which was distinctly of his own devising, thus becoming both prime mover and innovator in policy formulation, is beyond question. That he built on broad and powerful precedents inherited from his predecessors is equally indisputable. The question is compounded by the fact that appeasement, in the form of a definite policy approach to foreign affairs in Europe, sprang in part from an imprecise state of mind, a climate of opinion, in the creation of which a broad array of experiences and influences had played a part, over an extended period of time. The appeasement mentality cannot be dissected with scientific precision, but its early development can at least be described in general terms.

Most historians who have examined this matter are inclined to locate the potent, early formative influences in the context of Britain's experiences in the First World War, especially during 1918, and the peace treaty of Versailles. But one historian who has devoted a full book to the subject goes back considerably further in time. Martin Gilbert sees a state of mind conducive to appeasement developing from the time of the Crimean War (1854–56).[1] Denunciation of that miserable conflict, especially by John Bright and, indirectly, Richard Cobden (leading

[1] Gilbert, *The Roots of Appeasement*, pp. 4ff.

Liberal politicians in mid-nineteenth century Britain), laid a strong foundation for doubt about the morality of war and initiated a gradual transformation in British attitudes toward the acceptance of war as a legitimate instrument of national policy. Thus Gilbert asserts:

> The age when war was romantic, when alliances were skilfully manipulated for sudden gain, and patriotism was the ability to cheer on soldiers from the sidelines—that age was dying. The age of conciliation and reconciliation, compromise and barter, realizing one's own faults, seeing both sides of any dispute, giving as well as taking, conceding as well as demanding—that age, the age of appeasement, had begun.[2]

In the half century which followed, Europe in general was free from wars of conquest, excluding wars of national unity, which reflects, if not a broader disillusionment with military aggression, at least an increasing recognition of the risks and dangers inherent in its pursuit. The alliance system, initiated by Bismarck and embraced in time by others, was intended to promote acceptance of the status quo and a sense of general security, not of impending conflict. Overseas expansion certainly provided an effective outlet for those whose tastes still catered to martial glory, but even colonial conflicts were widely subjected to compromise settlement in the early years of the twentieth century. That this was due in part to growing anxiety about waxing German strength and bellicosity does not diminish the fact that a will to war was conspicuously absent throughout the continent of Europe in this particular period. Nor does the tense decade which preceded 1914 prove otherwise. Intense points of international conflict abounded, with no shortage of diplomatic crises. A game of power and prestige, influenced by nationalist exuberence and the perceived requirements of national security, was played by all the major nations. But it was widely assumed that diplomacy would succeed and peace would prevail, as if ordained by nature. And the seemingly successful settlement of potentially explosive troubles in the Balkans as late as 1913, by means of great power agreement reminiscent of the nineteenth-century Concert of Europe, lent weight to the aura of confidence.

The outbreak of war in early August 1914 came as a terrible shock to those, especially in Britain, who had placed their faith in diplomacy and come to think of war among modern civilized states as absurd and impossible. No amount of wartime propaganda, however effective in creating confidence in the nation's cause—the defence of Britain, and Europe, from a deliberate attempt at conquest—and a spirit of dedication to the honoured dead, could obliterate the nagging question 'why?' or destroy the lingering disillusionment, the sense of sheer futility in it all. Surely the cause of self-defence was just. But need the war have come at all? In the minds of those who doubted, who inclined

[2] Gilbert, *The Roots of Appeasement*, p. 5.

to explanations of accident and misunderstanding instead of clear necessity, and who resolved that nothing should be left undone in the future to prevent the recurrence of so tragic an error, appeasement attitudes germinated. Thus, as Gilbert writes: 'It was not the defeat of Germany in 1918, nor the severity of the peace terms in 1919, which created the first guilty consciences on which appeasement was to grow: it was the outbreak of war.'[3]

By the war's end, British opinion generally favoured a harsh peace. The course of conflict had hardened minds with hate and suspicion; suffering naturally spawned resentment; the Germans must pay the price of their folly. But this feeling was not as resolute as it appeared, accompanied as it was by an instinctive rejection of any part of the wartime experience which might imply new obligations. Utter exhaustion, physical, psychological, moral, ordained that outlook. Indeed, there emerged instead a marked reluctance to assume responsibility for terms of peace which would have to be enforced, a mood for which Wilsonian formulae, seeming to set moral action in perpetual motion with little need for continuing human supervision, seemed ready made. Thus the way was opened for the development of a mystique of peace by which simple laws of evidence and causation were ignored or twisted, and the danger of war was laid aside by the convenient method of self-hypnosis. But this is ahead of the story.

Within the British government there were doubts about the wisdom of a harsh treaty. The prime minister, Lloyd George, and some of his cabinet colleagues looked toward the coming peace conference with a surprising spirit of moderation, aware that treaties, gone awry, can create more problems than they resolve. Moderation, however, did not prevail at Versailles. Unable to move the French from revenge, and constrained by the vengeful mood which emerged in the British election campaign of December 1918, they were in no position to modify the treaty significantly according to their own predilections. The result was threefold for Britain—a peace treaty of which some leading Englishmen, especially politicians and publicists, disapproved; a basis for alienation among Britain and her recent allies; and grounds for the development of appeasement as a necessary corrective to an unwise and unjust settlement. So potent was the latter consideration that it became, in varying degrees, a vital element in the foreign policy of every prime minister in the years thereafter.

Appeasement was thus inextricably connected with Versailles. The treaty had its defenders, but from the moment of its signature was frontally attacked for the harsh treatment meted out to Germany. No criticism was more telling than that of economist John Maynard Keynes, whose book, *The Economic Consequences of the Peace*, was published late in 1919. This not only exerted tremendous influence through its excoriation of the economic unreality of Versailles, particularly German reparations

[3] Gilbert, *The Roots of Appeasement*, p. 11.

and the anticipated manner of their payment, but opened for public discussion previously muted feelings about the treaty. The result was devastating. The defenders of Versailles dwindled rapidly, especially among the educated. An uneasy feeling of guilt appeared. And as Keynes' foundation for doubt about the morality of war and initiated a gradual judgement was reinforced by other respected voices a significant segment of national sentiment naturally moved toward thoughts of treaty revision and 'making it up' to Germany.

The unyielding attachment of the French to strict enforcement of the treaty met with declining sympathy in Britain. By the time of the French occupation of the Ruhr in early 1923, following a German default in reparations payment, British impatience verged on genuine animosity. At that juncture the British mood was more anti-French than it was pro-German. But French 'folly' was a sharp spur to British sympathy for Germany and an important factor in stimulating a British frame of mind conducive to appeasement. Indeed, Anglo-French differences of outlook and policy, which characterized much of the inter-war period and appeared at times to border on alienation, weighed heavily on the minds of British policy-makers, eventually assuming major proportions in terms of perceived unreliability and distrust.[4]

Lloyd George, who remained in office until October 1922, sought to play a mediating role between France and Germany and thus an 'appeasing' role toward the latter. Instrumental in securing the abandonment of war crimes trials, which would only antagonize the German people, he also worked for the amelioration of France's reparations demands. He spoke out in favour of treating with Germany as an equal and attempting to reach through open negotiations a comprehensive settlement of European economic, and related, issues. This was not a matter of right and justice alone. There were some very practical reasons for Britain to adopt a moderate stance toward the defeated Germany. Mutual economic cooperation in a free trade atmosphere, to which reparations and war debts were awkward obstructions, was thought essential to the economic well-being of Europe, and Britain in particular. Further, the balance of world power was potentially unfavourable to Britain (and France) in the post-war years. She had emerged from war victorious in name, but her diminished resources, especially evident in the areas of naval power, economic strength, and Commonwealth relationships, dictated 'a technique of striving for composure rather than of framing a counterbalance against Germany'.[5] These limitations

---

[4] Anglo-French relations in the inter-war period are effectively detailed in Arnold Wolfers, *Britain and France between Two Wars: Conflicting Strategies of Peace since Versailles* (New York, 1940) and W. M. Jordan, *Great Britain, France, and the German Problem, 1918–1939* (London, 1943). Also very useful are pertinent sections of the more recent Neville Waites (editor), *Troubled Neighbours: Franco-British Relations in the Twentieth Century* (London, 1971).

[5] Northedge, *The Troubled Giant*, p. 624.

were not widely recognized at once, but came in time to exert a potent, if subtle, influence on policy formulation.

The prime ministers who succeeded Lloyd George, Bonar Law (1922–23), Stanley Baldwin (1923–24, 1924–29), and Ramsey MacDonald (1924, 1929–31) also thought in terms of general appeasement, though the term was not yet often used to characterize British policy. All three sought to ameliorate tempers, to mediate Franco-German differences, and to foster open negotiations for peaceful change. All perceived the indivisibility of economic recovery and political understanding, the latter best attained perhaps by Britain's pursuit of a 'neutral' policy designed to allay the security concerns which agitated both French and Germans. All encountered the serious obstacle of French intractability which, however understandable from France's particular vantage point, stood in the way of Germany's return to a 'normal' place in the affairs of Europe. And all experienced the frustration of Franco-German failure to appreciate their efforts, the Germans often seeing British policy as devoid of constructive content, the French as near betrayal.

But there were some successes which augured well. The Dawes plan, developed by a League of Nations committee in 1924, geared the discharge of Germany's reparations to her financial capacity and represented a victory for those who saw the reparations issue as basically economic, not political, in character. It was in large degree of British inspiration. Still more spectacularly, the Locarno agreements of October 1925, which included a five-power (France, Germany, Belgium, Britain, and Italy) guarantee of Germany's western boundaries and a series of bilateral arbitration conventions between Germany and other nations, introduced a new spirit of compromise and reconciliation into European affairs. It constituted, as foreign secretary Austen Chamberlain told the House of Commons on November 18th, 1925, only the beginning 'of the work of appeasement and reconciliation'.[6] Indeed, the years immediately following Locarno witnessed a variety of international conferences and agreements which seemed to lay the past aside and to look more confidently toward a future of European peace and stability. British initiative in these developments was modest; the nation was increasingly concerned with domestic problems and imperial affairs, and Baldwin was not intrigued by foreign relations. But a frame of mind favourable to appeasement was nonetheless present and developing, at least in government circles, even though the public was little involved or concerned, as it later came to be.

The emergence of Nazism at the beginning of the 1930s as a real political force in Germany seriously threatened to change the complexion of Europe in regard to the prospects for peace and stability. If Weimar Germany had thus far only grudgingly accepted the role in Europe

---

[6] *House of Commons Debates*, November 18th, 1925, col. 420.

decreed for it by Versailles, and worked with persistence and animadversion to alter its lot, how much more difficult would it be to deal with a German government led by a party already known, though perhaps not nearly well enough, for its blatant extremism? The upshot was a revived British interest in devising concessions which might at the same time strengthen moderate elements in Germany and advance international conciliation. MacDonald's Labour government fixed on disarmament as a means to accomplish this end and pursued it with diligence, though not success, until the eventual collapse of the World Disarmament Conference (1934). With the onset of severe economic crisis in 1931, there was talk of redressing German colonial grievances for the dual purpose of improving her economic condition and promoting political pacification. The emergence of the National government in late 1931 did not alter the direction of policy aspirations. Some prominent foreign office officials believed the time was right to confront directly treaty revision in order to head off German revolution and an eventual war of revenge, and there was more than a little support for their view. But the need for specific proposals which might bridge the gulf between Germany and France was easier to recognize than it was to meet, and in the ebb and flow of unsettled times and democratic debate nothing specific came forth.

The liquidation of reparations at the Lausanne conference (July 1932), where the impossibility of Germany's resumption of payments, after a year-long moratorium, was acknowledged by her European creditors, seemed a triumph for British objectives of conciliation. But the turmoil in German politics precluded any positive effect before Hitler became chancellor in January 1933. Clinched by the Enabling Act, which was passed by the Reichstag in late March and gave Hitler dictatorial power, this boded ill for the cause of reconciliation. With Germany slipping swiftly under the control of a frenzied demagogue who had long derided democratic diplomacy, British hopes for accommodation began to recede. Early accounts of Nazi domestic brutality prompted instead a mood of anxiety, abhorrence, and hostility. Hitler quickly became, in Britain, his own worst enemy by alienating a large segment of opinion which had earlier viewed with sympathy Germany's restoration to her 'rightful place' in Europe. Some of the newly disillusioned never recovered, and carried a conviction that it was impossible to do business with Hitler right up to the outbreak of war in 1939.[7] Many, however, gradually grew accustomed to the violence of the Nazi regime and adjusted to the idea that so long as the Nazis restricted to internal affairs their odious behaviour, sometimes dismissed as characteristically German, it might still be possible to deal with them

[7] Robert Vansittart is a prominent example. So pronounced did his anti-Germanism become that he was at length removed as permanent under-secretary in the foreign office by Neville Chamberlain, through the device of 'promoting' him to a newly created and powerless position of chief diplomatic adviser.

in the realm of foreign relations. Further, one potential way to feel out Hitler was to take him at his word, to offer satisfaction of his legitimate objectives, and thus to see whether this would have a calming effect. Since some early British visitors to Nazi Germany and to Hitler were inclined to think his bluster partly contrived for foreign consumption, experimentation in this direction seemed all the more appealing.

Nevertheless, there were no major policy initiatives in the direction of reconciliation with Germany for several years. A number of government officials, and the foreign office in particular, doubted the wisdom of seeking compromise with Hitler too quickly. In addition, preoccupation with a host of other problems, ranging from continuing economic dislocation to Japanese aggression in China, thrust Anglo-German relations into the background. It was not until the spring of 1935 that specific steps in the direction of appeasement were taken again.

In response to an Anglo-French suggestion in February that Locarno should be supplemented by an air pact, under which each Locarno power would render air assistance to any other of their number attacked from the air, Germany agreed to examine this and other proposals with the British government. To the alarm of the French, Simon, the foreign secretary, and Eden, minister for League of Nations affairs, visited Berlin on March 25th, after delay and confusion occasioned by the German announcement of rearmament on March 16th—the first open violation of the Versailles Treaty but an event widely interpreted in Britain as the inevitable consequence of the failure of the World Disarmament Conference. Though no air pact resulted, information exchanged led to the swift, surprising negotiation of an Anglo-German naval agreement in London in June.

That agreement, which authorized for Germany a navy one-third the size of Britain's and full parity with the Commonwealth in submarines, seemed to embody convincing testimony of British intentions to revise Versailles. From one point of view, it appeared to be a tribute to British realism and common sense. Whereas France's refusal to compromise had led to unlimited German rearmament on land, Britain, by her more conciliatory attitude, had secured an important limitation on German naval strength, if Hitler's word could be trusted. It constituted a potential triumph for the cause of appeasement. But it was also highly provocative in its revision of Versailles without consulting other treaty signatories and with little apparent regard for French, Italian, and Russian sensitivities. Coming on the heels of a British-sponsored resolution at Geneva, protesting against Germany's intention to rearm in defiance of Versailles, its inconsistency was bewildering. And its tempering effect on the course of future German policy could only be conjectured.

The force of appeasement attitudes was also intermittently apparent in Britain's response to Italy's aggression against Abyssinia during 1935–36. Though incensed by Italian crudity and alarmed at the threat to British colonial interests, and at length impelled to lead in the enacting (by the League of Nations council) of economic sanctions against Italy, the British government sought industriously over a period of months during 1935 for a diplomatic bargain behind the scenes. Its objects were to satisfy Italian demands for land and glory and to extricate Italy from an awkward situation of her own making in such a way as to avoid alienating her as a potential ally in Europe. The infamous Hoare-Laval plan, by which Italy would have acquired two-thirds of Abyssinia and a virtual protectorate over the rest, while the Abyssinians would be bought off with a corridor to the sea through British Somaliland, was but the unfortunate culmination of British efforts to arrange a settlement at Abyssinian, and their own, expense. On the other hand, the outraged public rejection of the plan, when it was prematurely leaked, showed that there were definite limits to which such concession-making could go.

Britain's response to Germany's remilitarization of the Rhineland (March 7th, 1936), now frequently identified as the turning point in Hitler's career of aggression, marks the epitome of passive appeasement. Though the government protested this unilateral and illegal violation of solemn international agreements, there was never any question of taking action to reverse it. The idea of military retaliation was overwhelmingly rejected and a half-hearted French suggestion of sanctions was brushed quickly aside. The British, in fact, felt a general measure of sympathy for Germany, both in terms of the harmlessness of her occupying "her own back yard" and of her stated objections to the Franco-Soviet mutual defence pact, recently ratified by the French Chamber of Deputies, as implying the encirclement of Germany. The best that Baldwin could do in the House of Commons on March 9th was to promise British support for France and Belgium against German attack, adding: 'In Europe we have no more desire than to keep calm, to keep our heads and to continue to try to bring France and Germany together in a friendship with ourselves.'[8]

During the nearly two years in which Baldwin headed the National government (1935–37), appeasement, especially of an economic variety, appeared to be the most potentially constructive policy approach to Germany. Serious discussion revolved around the wide-ranging proposals for Anglo-German cooperation advanced by Frank Ashton-Gwatkin, first head of the new economic section in the foreign office. These proposals ranged from a mutual reduction of tariffs and import quotas to the formation of an Anglo-German economic bloc and even the inclusion of Germany in a full-blown, European-wide common market. Behind them all lay the hope and conviction that a reduction of unnatural economic barriers would relax political pressures, and specific Anglo-German economic arrangements would open the way for

    [8] *House of Commons Debates*, March 9th, 1936, col. 1841. See Maurice Baumont, 'The Rhineland Crisis: March 7th, 1936', in Waites, *Troubled Neighbours*.

political understanding. Germany might come to understand that prosperity could be won by peaceful means, a realization of inestimable benefit to all Europe. Little tangible result came from this, however. British suggestions, quietly advanced when convenient occasions arose, stirred next to no response in Germany. Economic appeasement remained, therefore, in the realm of future possibility, reserved with hope for a more propitious time.

One of those who did not believe that progress in economic cooperation would necessarily soothe political tension was Neville Chamberlain. His experience in international monetary negotiations as chancellor of the exchequer since 1931 did not bear out that conclusion. Not surprisingly, then, especially in view of Germany's apparent disinterest in economic proposals, his early efforts at appeasement were directed more toward the political realm.

This brief survey of Britain's policy outlook, particularly toward Germany from the First World War to 1937, reveals a steady, if somewhat uneven, awareness of legitimate German grievances and an honest concern to negotiate them, thus restoring Germany to her 'rightful place' in Europe, enhancing continental stability, and, not incidentally, creating an atmosphere in which the problems of economic and social progress might command first attention. A basic sense of appeasement, of placation and pacification, pervaded and conditioned British policy during these years, even though the policy approach it embodied was not so labelled with any regularity before the mid-1930s. The pursuit of appeasement was, until 1937, more passive than active; efforts to apply appeasing techniques and policies developed piecemeal in response to occasional opportunities which arose in the general course of events. There was no effort to formulate a well defined 'programme' for appeasement or to launch a campaign for its attainment. That was left to Chamberlain, whose initiatives in this regard reflected both the temperament of the man and the intensified urgency of the situation in which he found himself.

Appeasement sentiment during this period was not restricted by political affiliation, economic class, educational level, social status or any other identifiable category among the English people. It claimed adherents in all parties and classes to such a degree that it seemed clearly to embody the national will. To a very impressive extent, appeasement represented an attitude of mind and a mode of human conduct considered not simply appropriate but genuinely essential to civilized life after the Great War by a very wide range of English opinion. Even the critics of appeasement, of whom there were few before 1937, were not inclined to charge that the policy was wrong in its basic intent and nature. Rather, it was mainly a question of whether it could in fact accomplish its objective without seriously endangering and shamefully demeaning the nation—or even accomplish it at all. On that issue, controversy waxed intense during the Chamberlain years. But it was only as evidence accumulated that Hitler and Mussolini, and the movements which they headed, were special cases that could not be handled by means which would normally soothe and control more rational men that the policy came to be questioned, attacked, and at length discredited in the eyes of a large segment of the population. And many were unduly slow to interpret the accumulating evidence as pointing toward a conclusion which they dearly hoped to avoid.

4 Motive Forces behind Appeasement

The forces and influences which pointed toward appeasement as the proper British policy attitude in the early 1920s seemed, on the surface at least, few and uncomplicated. But they grew in number and complexity with the passing of time, the changing of circumstances, and the appearance of new personalities until appeasement in the Chamberlain era became a phenomenon of manifold motivation. Some of these forces were broadly related to the movement of English and European history over several decades and more of time; some were essentially unique to the Chamberlain period. Some were widely influential on many people, though with varying degrees of intensity at different points in time. Others were narrowly influential, but important in the minds of persons in positions of power and responsibility. Some were practical, some theoretical; some were substantive, some procedural; some were rational, some emotional. In combinations of varying proportions, not easily measurable in the minds of most appeasers, they subtly fused into a general conviction of 'right'.

Of all the factors in British appeasement, none was more potent than the abhorrence of war as a means of settling international difficulties in the twentieth century. Surely the historical lesson of the First World War was clearly writ: the total nature of that great struggle had rendered war in its traditional role as senseless beyond contemplation. It was not that the whole nation had converted to philosophical pacifism, for only a wing of the Labour party had taken that route. Nor was it a matter of cowardice, irresponsibility, or fear. It was simply a poignant realization of the terrible destruction wrought by modern war; a keen appreciation that its costs vastly exceeded any benefits which might accrue to a prospective victor, in name only; a plain recognition that Europe had reached a stage of moral development where war must be considered a barbarity incompatible with civilized life; and a deeper commitment to rationality as the foundation stone of human behaviour. War, in short, had emerged in the British mind as the ultimate evil. Nothing would justify another one.

Widely felt by Englishmen of all conditions and persuasions,[1] these

---

[1] The so-called 'peace ballot' of 1935, however indecisive as an expression of national determination, was widely taken as conclusive evidence, if that were needed, of the overwhelmingly peaceful sentiments of the English people.

views found especially keen expression in the person of Neville Chamberlain during his premiership. He constantly stressed the futility of conflict and asserted that only the 'big issues', which he never defined, but apparently meant the domination of Europe by a single power or direct attack on Britain's vital interests, conservatively perceived, would warrant the use of war. Thus he conveyed an impression of British opinion at once both admirable in its commitment to peace and dangerous in purveying to potential aggressors a notion of British decline and consequent inability to stand up for anyone or anything. But his conviction was firm. The literal decimation of a generation of young men by the holocaust of 1914–18 had left a lasting impression on him, one which was constantly reinforced as he scanned in vain the back benches of parliament for younger party members of talent.[2] He had been thoroughly shaken by the loss in battle of his cousin Norman, one of his few close friends and a promising Chamberlain standard bearer of the future. He was assuredly a 'man of peace', and in this sense representative of an overwhelming majority of Englishmen.

In view of this climate of opinion, the concept of appeasement had an inherent strength and appeal which was widely felt and accepted without questioning. It was Christian to deal charitably with one's neighbour. It was civilized and humane to show patience, tolerance, and generosity toward a defeated enemy. It was also good diplomacy, in that it aimed to remove the bases for bitterness and revenge upon which dangerous estrangement could feed. If the avoidance of war was the highest ambition of statemanship, a verity widely accepted by generations of statesmen, the placation of an adversary was a fundamental purpose of all diplomacy, a necessary condition of the civilized order which that diplomacy was intended to preserve and develop.[3] Appeasement 'made sense' as offering the most likely prospect for reducing hostility and returning Europe to stable, peaceful ways. By the late 1930s, the internal excesses of the Nazi regime, as well as its external blustering, began to disturb the feeling of charity toward Germany. But an attitude so deeply rooted faded very slowly, especially when constantly nourished by Chamberlain, who persisted long in the vain belief that proper adjustments in Germany's European condition would still result in German satisfaction and goodwill. This was reflected in the experience of the more alert and sceptical segments of the British press, which found it 'both financially and intellectually . . . unwise or impossible . . . to adopt a strongly critical line towards Nazi Germany; the readers did not want to read it, and the intellectuals did not want to write it.'[4]

Behind all this lay the fact that appeasement fed on an attitude of sympathy for Germany, even, to some degree, an active pro-Germanism,

[2] There was, no doubt, more talent than Chamberlain perceived; it just did not fit his particular scheme of things at that juncture.
[3] John W. Wheeler-Bennett, *Munich: Prologue to Tragedy* (London, 1948), p. 3.
[4] Franklin R. Gannon, *The British Press and Germany, 1936–1939* (Oxford, 1971), p. 2.

a state of mind itself of fairly complicated and long-term origin. There was, of course, first and foremost, the matter of Versailles and the sense of guilt which prompted Englishmen to view Germany's plight, presumed or real, in such a way as always to give Germany the benefit of the doubt. If the psychological situation made another war unthinkable in a general sense, the discrediting of Versailles made still more senseless the idea of a war against Germany for trying to revise the treaty. There was also the dictate of economic reality, in that a revived and prosperous Germany was vital to British economic well-being. And Germany, under Nazi control, did begin to revive. Numerous British visitors in the early years of the Nazi regime returned with glowing reports of Germany's gathering vitality. These and favourable press accounts generated a certain appreciation for the Germans' ability to 'get things done'; and the oft-repeated (especially in Conservative circles) slogan of 1936–37, 'Better Hitler than Blum', expressed a preference for Germany's disciplined efforts as compared to France's slovenly languishing under left-wing politicians. Beyond all this, there was in some quarters a subtle acceptance of an Anglo-German affinity rooted in deep historical origins, racial identity, cultural association and shared characteristics, including a common concern for inner discipline, honest labour, and effective national power. The latter considerations hardly moved the mass of English people, but they wielded considerable influence among the educated element, the social, economic, and political leaders. And they were reinforced by a belief, fostered alike by British historians and German propagandists, in basic Anglo-German responsibility for the First World War—the idea that different courses of action by those two nations could have averted that catastrophe—and the feeling that, in combination, it was quite within their power still to control the European situation to their mutual benefit.

By the time of Chamberlain's accession, there had developed in Britain an extensive appreciation of Germany's 'legitimate interests' (a description often used) in Europe, and especially in eastern Europe. Initially conceived in terms more economic and commercial than territorial or political, distinctions were neither carefully nor easily drawn. Indeed, acceptance of the principle of dominant German influence in eastern Europe was basic to Chamberlain's policy. It was considered a wholly natural thing. Anyway, very little could be done to prevent it and diplomacy ought not be set a task obviously beyond attainment. If British commercial interests were not endangered and the power structure of western Europe left unimpaired, Britain could object little to Germany's search for fulfilment in the east of Europe. The extent to which this British view was a natural culmination of earlier pro-German sentiment, as opposed to the blunt acknowledgment of power realities, is hard to say; certainly the former made the latter more readily acceptable.

The element of pro-German feeling in Britain was matched, indeed in some ways conditioned by, an equal element of anti-French sentiment. That, too, was an important factor in the shaping of appeasement attitudes. Their close association in the great crusade of 1914–18 or, in broader terms, their common fear of an expansive Germany since 1900, as well as their common ideological posture, tended to emphasize a unity in Anglo-French relations which obscured their differing perceptions of certain European problems. The differences surfaced with shocking suddenness once the war was over. The French insistence on German debilitation as a means of ensuring their own security did not correspond with British interests in a revitalized Germany capable of vigorous trade. Nor did it agree with the British perception of fair play and benevolence toward the defeated enemy. There developed, in consequence, a widening, if fluctuating, rift in Anglo-French relations which persisted throughout the inter-war period, rendering that relationship considerably less than an amiable, steady, and confident association of victorious allies.

It was not simply a matter of policy differences. It became, in time, a matter of deteriorating national empathy. The British, as John Cairns has recently written, 'evidently never quite knew what to make of France: she was too weak or too strong, too independent or too obviously dependent, too much a reminder of the bloody past, too much a warning, with her alliances, of possible troubles to come.'[5] The familiar problems of French domestic politics compounded matters until there developed in Britain a thorough lack of confidence in French stability, strength, and consequent value as a steadying force in the European order. The proclivity of French statesmen for resolute public pronouncements which they regularly, almost methodically, countered with equivocal private statements naturally engendered consternation, suspicion, and distrust among British officials.[6] Chamberlain and many of his colleagues had a generally low regard for the quality of French statesmen and statesmanship, and were not always mistaken in their judgements. He felt little confidence in France's willingness or ability to stand up to Germany, or to deal with her in any effective way, and became concerned largely with the possibility that French ministers, in a moment of tension and under mounting public pressure to 'do something', might end up doing something very silly, thus dashing his own hopes or destroying his own efforts at appeasement. The upshot was British dominance in Anglo-French initiatives in the years 1938–39, one element of which was the regular summoning of French ministers to London for consultation, and the general subordination of French foreign policy to Britain's. That British doubts about France's strength and determina-

---

[5] John C. Cairns, 'A Nation of Shopkeepers in Search of a Suitable France: 1919–1940', *American Historical Review* LXXIX, no. 3 (1974), p. 729.
[6] See Lord Butler, *The Art of the Possible: the Memoirs of Lord Butler* (London, 1971), p. 68.

tion, and the inclination to browbeat the French to accept the British view of things, may have reflected Britain's own position of weakness cannot be summarily rejected.[7] Nor can the possibility be ignored that French policy might have been different had greater support for firmness issued from Britain at critical moments. But whatever the judgement of history on these matters, Britain's lack of faith in France was another spur to appeasement.

Britain's military condition in the inter-war period strongly influenced appeasement, though it is nearly impossible to say how decisive it was at critical points in the Chamberlain years. Itself the result of a complex of forces ranging from the moral revulsion against war to a keen, practical resentment against expending on armaments financial resources desperately needed for domestic programmes, the nation's military posture was dangerously weak as the threat of German aggression developed. During the 1920s, Britain had clung tenaciously to hopes for world disarmament through the League of Nations, and in spite of French recalcitrance, had made persistent efforts to promote that purpose. She was a central participant in successful conferences on the reduction of naval armaments, held at Washington (1922) and London (1930). She took a lead in beating down French proposals in the League of Nations council which would have given precedence over disarmament to schemes for military action against aggressors, acting in part, no doubt, from her traditional refusal to undertake specific prior commitments on the European continent. She played a leading role in the preparatory commission for the World Disarmament Conference during the later 1920s and was more diligent than any other nation both in devising draft documents for consideration by the commission, and later the conference itself (1932–34), and in attempting to revise rejected drafts so as to meet the objections raised by dissenting nations in conference deliberations.

This strong commitment to disarmament was not easily discarded when the World Disarmament Conference failed and the bluster of totalitarian dictators began to put the issue of rearmament in somewhat different perspective. Indeed, it became a biting issue in domestic politics: the Labour party staunchly resisted, and branded as warmongering, modest Conservative proposals to repair perceived deficiencies, and all the while called for active British participation in schemes for collective security; the Conservatives cautiously advanced proposals on the understanding that armaments so provided for minimal deterrent action would not be used to involve the nation in continental adventures. Ironically, in his role as chancellor of the exchequer,

[7] See Cairns, 'A Nation of Shopkeepers', pp. 735–6. At the same time, there seems to have been very good reason for British doubts. See Anthony Adamthwaite, 'Reactions to the Munich Crisis', in Waites, *Troubled Neighbours*. Arthur H. Furnia, in *The Diplomacy of Appeasement: Anglo-French Relations and the Prelude to World War II, 1931–1938* (Washington, 1960), seems to overemphasize British duplicity toward the French. Of special note is the recent *Les Relations Franco-Brittaniques de 1935 à 1939* (Paris, 1975).

Chamberlain did more than any other minister to promote rearmament, through the development and submission of white papers on defence during 1935–37. But the nation's efforts were wholly inadequate.[8] By the time he became prime minister, British plans were still largely in the drawing board stage and, convinced as he was that policy must depend on power, this fact surely influenced his foreign policy outlook.

When, at the end of 1937, the chiefs of staff prepared a memorandum comparing the strength of Britain with other nations, they observed that the time was far distant when British defence forces would be able to safeguard the nation's territory, trade, and vital interests against Germany, Italy, and Japan simultaneously. In consequence, they added, 'we cannot . . . exaggerate the importance . . . of any political or international action that can be taken to reduce the numbers of our potential enemies and to gain the support of potential allies.'[9] Coming as it did amid a tide of treasury warnings lest substantially increased rearmament expenditure, embodied in the service estimates, disrupt the gathering economic resilience of the nation, this report also reinforced Chamberlain's hopes for active appeasement. When cabinet discussion of the memorandum emphasized that the limitations imposed on defence by finance placed a heavy burden on diplomacy, Halifax drew the clear conclusion: 'we ought to make every possible effort to get on good terms with Germany.'[10] Thus 1937 closed with British hopes pinned to diplomacy alone and military preparedness still subservient to the principle of non-interference with the normal operations of British finance and industry.

Nor did much change occur during 1938. Reviewing the military situation immediately after the *Anschluss*, the chiefs of staff found the nation quite unprepared for war, to the point of advising that war with Germany over Czechoslovakia must be avoided, no matter what the cost, until the rearmament programme began to bear 'substantial fruit'.[11] General Ironside, later chief of the imperial general staff, recorded in his diary on March 29th: 'The paper on our rearmament . . . is truly the most appalling reading. How we can have come to this state is beyond believing. . . . No foreign nation would believe it.'[12] This was the military background against which cabinet policy toward Czechoslovakia was formulated. As the Czech crisis unfolded, other considerations, including disbelief that the Czech-Sudeten German

[8] Peter Dennis, *Decision by Default: Peacetime Conscription and British Defence, 1919–1939* (Durham, 1972), graphically portrays the confused and inadequate planning for British defence.

[9] Colvin, *The Chamberlain Cabinet*, pp. 62–4. The reaction of the foreign office was that 'it might be more in keeping with our honour and dignity to pursue a policy of armed strength'. *ibid.*, pp. 66–7.

[10] *ibid.*, p. 79. Cabinet concern with the crippling cost of rearmament is shown in Middlemas, *Diplomacy of Illusion*, pp. 110ff.

[11] P. K. Kemp, *Key to Victory: the Triumph of British Sea Power in World War II* (Boston, 1957), p. 26.

[12] Roderick Macleod and Denis Kelly (editors), *The Ironside Diaries, 1937–1940* (London, 1962), pp. 53–4.

issue was worth a European war, gained ascendancy over questions of military preparedness in the minds of Chamberlain and British policy-makers. And Chamberlain, unlike some of his colleagues, was convinced that the policy which culminated in Munich was 'right', aside from any dictates borne of military necessity. But the issue of military weakness was always there, lurking in the background and weighing uncertainly in the minds of those who, like Halifax, were truly alarmed by Hitler's tactics but who saw Munich, 'a horrible and wretched business', as still the lesser of evils.[13] This condition did not begin to change appreciably until the spring of 1939, while the degree of change and its consequent implications for policy formulation remained even then a matter of controversy subject to varying interpretations.

Throughout these years it was not so much a failure to recognize potential dangers involved in the nation's military weakness which lay at the root of the problem, for these were increasingly conceded by a widening circle of observers. It was rather extreme reluctance to believe the European situation yet nasty enough to warrant an emergency commitment to rearmament on a veritable crash basis, with all the sacrifices which that would surely entail. In its slowness to grasp reality here, the entire English nation fell short, the government bearing a special responsibility, of course, because it showed no disposition to inform and lead.

In view of her acknowledged military weakness and the lingering emphasis on collective security, which had been the byword of European diplomacy from 1920 to the mid-1930s, Britain might have looked to the League of Nations for succour and support in a time of deepening international tensions. She did not, after 1935, and her lack of confidence in the League's ability to serve effectively the chief function for which it had been created constituted another incentive to go-it-alone appeasement. The British had never envisaged the League as the potent agency for action against aggressors which some other nations, notably France, had hoped it might be. Its dismal failure to take effective action when confronted with Japanese aggression in Manchuria seemed to confirm British doubts about its usefulness in this particular role; and the disastrous collapse of its efforts to halt Italian aggression in Ethiopia, after the British had played a leading role in instituting economic sanctions to serve that end, was a most disheartening experience. Chamberlain frankly acknowledged his own loss of confidence in the League and collective security, and nothing happened to change his mind thereafter. It was not only that the League had demonstrated its incapacity to handle critical situations; the aggrieved powers of Europe, Germany and Italy, were no longer members, and persisted in seeing it as a tool for blocking the attainment of their legitimate objectives. How, then, could differences be composed under auspices of the League of Nations? Chamberlain was, in time, subjected

---

[13] Lord Halifax, *Fullness of Days* (New York, 1957), p. 201.

to bitter criticism by the Labour party, which continued to put its faith in the League and collective security, though unwilling to support the rearmament essential for Britain to make an effective contribution to it; and a few Conservatives pushed for a revitalized League which might assume, with British support and initiative, a much more responsible role in the affairs of Europe. To the latter idea Chamberlain and his colleagues offered occasional lip-service but nothing more, preferring to tackle the pressing problems of international relations via the 'new' techniques of appeasement.

With the League discredited in the eyes of the Chamberlain government, the matter of Commonwealth attitudes toward Britain's position in European affairs took on added potential importance. It is difficult to gauge the weight attached to this, especially since it sometimes appears that the government was inclined to utilize dominion sentiment at least as much to provide reinforcement and justification for the course on which it was already set than as an influencing factor in determining its policy. But frequent government references to dominion attitudes suggest that it was an ever present element, and one which lent support of no mean proportions to the efforts toward appeasement.

The dominions were, in general, extremely cool toward any British involvement in Europe which might affect the nation's capacity to come to their own defence, or conversely, imply the slightest need of their support for a Britain unnecessarily enmeshed in European entanglements. This posture was not new; it had characterized the dominions' outlook since their opposition to Locarno in 1925. The London Imperial Conference of mid-1937 reaffirmed it, Malcolm MacDonald (dominions secretary) reporting to the cabinet the Commonwealth prime ministers' definite inclination 'to look rather more critically at British involvement in Europe than His Majesty's Government itself cared to'. And there was no disposition to give support to Britain in any case that did not involve a direct threat to her very existence.[14] Later, as the Czech crisis developed during 1938, the dominions not only stood squarely against the idea of war over Czechoslovakia, but had no sympathy whatever for a British commitment to France covering German aggression against the Czechs. The Munich 'solution' to the Czechoslovak problem was warmly greeted throughout the Commonwealth, as it was in fact, at least momentarily, throughout the world. And while Hitler's seizure of Prague (March 1939) prompted clear expressions of disgust and anxiety, only Australia approved the British guarantee to Poland. During the summer of 1939 there was lingering hope that a British agreement with Russia, for which there was no great enthusiasm, might nonetheless facilitate renewal of the search for appeasement; and the final Polish crisis was marked by an inclination to give Germany every benefit of doubt in the hope of attaining a negotiated settlement. Thus dominion sentiment was characterized by isolationist attitudes, a stance against

[14] Colvin, *The Chamberlain Cabinet*, pp. 43–4.

involvement which lent support to British efforts to attain appeasement and thus avoid entangling arrangements of any kind. This must have been to the government's liking; no effort was made to influence dominion sentiment in other directions or to encourage dominion ministers to see the British role in Europe's affairs from any other perspective.[15]

Still more difficult to weigh is the role of American influence on appeasement, particularly the effect of the British government's perception of America's 'sense of responsibility' and potential for involvement in Europe. Like the matter of Commonwealth sentiment, however, America's position in international affairs surfaced in British discussions with regularity sufficient to suggest that it was a factor in British calculations. The question usually arose whenever alternatives to appeasement were canvassed, especially when the government came under opposition fire for failing to rally the support of other nations in a stiffer policy of resistance to Germany. And the conclusion reached in government circles, not without occasional dissent, was invariably the same: the United States could not be counted on to involve itself in the affairs of Europe or even to exercise its influence in potentially effective ways. That being so, a British policy which proceeded without resort to American support of any kind seemed reasonable and essential. Appeasement was such a policy.

Chamberlain was as wary as anyone of taking America into British foreign policy calculations. This was partly the result of earlier experiences in dealing with irresponsible (as he saw it) American attitudes and policies on international monetary matters, as well as sharp resentment of the anti-British accent which accompanied the isolationist tone of much of the American press; but mainly it involved a plain conviction that, in view of the strength of American isolationist sentiment, there was simply no way in which the United States would intervene in the problems facing Europe. Even should President Roosevelt try it, congress would never approve of resolute intervention. The foreign secretary, Anthony Eden, was one minister who placed a more positive evaluation on America's potential role in Europe and stressed the need to foster it. But Eden stood alone. 'Rightly or wrongly', Sir Samuel Hoare, the home secretary, later attested, most leading ministers 'were deeply suspicious . . . of American readiness to follow up inspiring words with any practical action' and thus were convinced that 'we must for the time being rely chiefly upon ourselves in the immed-

[15] For detail on dominion sentiment, see D. C. Watt, *Personalities and Policies: Studies in the Formulation of British Foreign Policy in the Twentieth Century* (Notre Dame, 1965), pp. 159–74; and Nicholas Mansergh, *Survey of British Commonwealth Affairs: Problems of External Policy, 1931–1939* (London, 1952), pp. 437–44. Pertinent material may also be found in Nicholas Mansergh (editor), *Documents and Speeches on British Commonwealth Affairs, 1931–1952* I (2 vols, London, 1953); and Gwendolyn M. Carter *The British Commonwealth and International Security: the Role of the Dominions, 1919–1939* (Toronto, 1947).

iate crisis that was facing Europe.'[16] That appraisal did not materially change until appeasement had long been drowned in the flood of war, at length necessitating drastic revisions of outlook on both sides of the Atlantic.

Of considerable importance among the factors buttressing the government's commitment to appeasement was its attitude toward Russia. Accepting her status as a great power with only the greatest reluctance, and viewing her distrustfully both in terms of ideology and practical politics, the Conservative-dominated governments of the 1930s were prepared first to ignore the Soviet Union, as much as possible, and later to go to very great lengths in pursuit of solutions to Europe's problems which would not involve Russian participation. Chamberlain saw the peace of Europe resting on friendly discussions among Britain, France, Italy, and Germany. Russia was excluded; her involvement would recreate the circumstances of 1914, effecting an encirclement which might be Hitler's pretext for an early war. Thus the possibility of co-operation with Russia, in dealing with German resurgence and potential aggression in central Europe, was ruled out sometime before the crises of 1938 developed. And time changed things but little. The Russian appeal for an international conference immediately after the *Anschluss* was dismissed as 'premature' without even so much as cabinet consideration.[17] Russia was not invited to Munich, despite her obvious vital interest and her pact of mutual defence with Czechoslovakia. Her reiterated appeal, upon the German conquest of Prague in March 1939, for a conference of Britain, France, Russia, Poland, Rumania, and Turkey to discuss the possibilities of common action was also lightly rejected.[18] Only when the most pressing circumstances, both international and domestic, left it no viable alternative did the Chamberlain government move reluctantly to open conversations with the Soviet Union in mid-April 1939; and the faltering course of those negotiations continued to reveal, right up to their fateful demise, a persistent doubt about the wisdom of association with Russia.

Behind this view of Russia lay an inextricable combination of ideological prejudice and honest political judgements. For many Conservative ministers, hatred and fear of Bolshevism, with its subversive doctrines of world revolution and socialism, had so conditioned their thinking that nearly everything for which the Soviet Union stood seemed antagonistic

---

[16] Templewood, *Nine Troubled Years*, p. 263. Chamberlain no doubt wanted America's support and understanding, but believed it safe to count on her for nothing but words. Roosevelt seems to have appeared to the British government as 'an unreliable windbag.' See Donald Watt, 'Roosevelt and Neville Chamberlain: Two Appeasers', *International Journal* xxviii, no. 2 (1973), pp. 185ff. Watt concludes that, had Roosevelt and Chamberlain been in opposite places, there would not have been much difference in their policy.

[17] Middlemas, *Diplomacy of Illusion*, p. 200.

[18] See above, p. 19.

and dangerous to traditional British values.[19] It seldom appeared expressly either in public statements or private deliberations, but an anti-communist disposition was never far beneath the surface of appeasement. Chamberlain acknowledged, from time to time, his profound distrust of Russia's motives and never altered his basic suspicion that behind every Russian initiative lay a mischief-making scheme to provoke, at worst, a deadly bourgeois war between the western democracies and Germany, at best, a recondite confusion conducive to the pursuit of her own selfish ends. Nor was he ever pressed by a significant number of cabinet colleagues to revise his negative appraisal.[20]

On the practical side, Russia was thought to be weak militarily, the result in part of a series of purges in which the general staff was especially hard hit.[21] In mid-summer 1939, Russia was still considered a less valuable military ally than Poland, and as Polish intransigence reinforced Britain's reluctance to collaborate with Russia, it was deemed best to make sure of Poland and leave the support of Russia to be sought, if necessary, at a later time. The prospects of political stability, ethical judgements of Soviet dictatorship aside, were not adjudged much better. The political purges had left a legacy of hate and confusion which, it was thought, precluded political cohesion and administrative efficiency for an extended period of time. And the economic travail of the nation as it struggled with agricultural and industrial modernization was generally taken to be far from ending. Consequently, Russia was simply not regarded as a worthy ally whose assistance would be crucial; and a policy which would solve the problems of central Europe without involving her seemed the wisest course of action. If such a policy would increase Russia's isolation and strengthen the barrier to potential communist penetration into eastern Europe, so much the better. Appeasement, again, was perceived by the Chamberlain government to be such a policy.

In contrast to the government's perception of Russia's motives, it is possible to see a notion of moral superiority lurking behind British

[19] The extent to which the danger was perceived as more narrowly personal than more generally societal is both disputable and irresolvable. But the contention that Conservative leaders calculated appeasement as a means of protecting their own class interests and privileges, raised in Margaret George, *The Warped Vision: British Foreign Policy, 1933–1939* (Pittsburgh, 1965), seems to stretch points of devious calculation and selfish motivation somewhat too far. Likewise, the view that Munich was a logical step in a frantic British crusade of anti-Bolshevism, a 'conspiracy for aggression' against Russia, advanced in Andrew Rothstein, *The Munich Conspiracy* (London, 1958), grossly exaggerates one of many factors which figured prominently in the formulation of British policy. This latter view is specifically rejected in Donald Lammers, *Explaining Munich: the Search for Motive in British Policy* (Stanford, 1966).

[20] Public opinion, admittedly hard to measure, was more favourably disposed to Russia; and pressure generated in sections of parliament and the press was instrumental in forcing the government to begin negotiations with Russia in April 1939. See Gannon, *The British Press and Germany, 1936–1939*, pp. 27–8, and Rock, *Appeasement on Trial*, pp. 252ff.

[21] See J. G. Purves, 'British Estimates of Soviet Military Strength', *New Review: A Journal of East-European History* VII, no. 4 (1967), pp. 1–10.

appeasement which might be counted among the factors from which the policy drew inspiration. Long a satisfied nation which wished only to maintain what it already had and to strengthen the peace and stability essential to business prosperity, Britain had risen above the factious struggles of other, perhaps lesser, peoples who still groped vainly for a proper place in the European order. Indeed, from her position of calm detachment, she had a special role to play in soothing the life of Europe. The cruder aspects of German and Italian behaviour were sometimes hard to tolerate, but Britain must abide their irascible conduct much as an understanding mother suffers the misbehaviour of an impish offspring until it reaches sufficient maturity to respond more fittingly. Only this sort of attitude can explain the consistent over-looking of unpalatable judgements on the nature of the Nazi menace which otherwise would have pointed policy in some very different direction.

Since appeasement in practice was so interconnected with the fate of Czechoslovakia, the British attitude toward that small nation merits consideration among the factors on which appeasement fed. The government's concern for Czechoslovak integrity was slight indeed. In reality, it saw only one way of settling the Sudeten German problem: for the Czechs to accept all Nazi demands whatever their consequences.[22] This conclusion followed easily upon the conspicuous absence of sympathy for the hodge-podge nation and a firm conviction that it could not be maintained intact even by a victorious war. The British were wont to accept complaints about Czech intransigence without examining their validity, to receive the explanations of Sudeten German leaders without challenge, and to ignore the possibility that Hitler might have moved against Czechoslovakia even had she not a single German within her borders. The Runciman report was 'doctored' by Chamberlain; no regard was shown for those Sudeten Germans, mainly Social Democrats, who supported Czech democracy and feared incorporation into Nazi Germany; Chamberlain, after Godesberg, trusted, or at least pretended to trust, Hitler more than after Berchtes-gaden; the prime minister, a stickler for administrative efficiency, jumped at the chance to deal with Hitler in a totally unplanned con-ference at Munich (no chairman, no agenda, no rules of procedure, no arrangment for minutes, not even ink in the inkwells when the time came to sign the agreement); and the British government assuaged its con-science by promising a vague and unworkable guarantee to rump Czechoslovakia—all these things point to the conclusion that the Czechoslovak issue was never weighed on its own merits.[23] The im-portant point was to pacify Hitler, and if Czechoslovakia had to be sacrificed in the process, so it must be. Surely she was not worth a war.

[22] This is a basic theme in J. W. Bruegel, *Czechoslovakia Before Munich: the German Minority Problem and British Appeasement Policy* (Cambridge, 1973), pp. 195ff.
[23] *ibid.*, pp. 209–19, 270, 274–85, 290–94, 300.

The British attitude toward Poland was not much different. The German case over Danzig and the Corridor was stronger than that over the Sudetenland. Moreover, to British public opinion Poland was the least attractive of the succession states, and had Hitler forced a settlement with Poland first, it is doubtful whether Britain, or France, would have raised a finger to help her.[24] The guarantee to Poland in late March 1939, had nothing to do with the merits of the German case or sympathy for the Poles. Rather, it sprang from a sudden and enforced recognition that Hitler's ambitions exceeded the rectification of grievances and from the imperative need for Britain to do something to demonstrate her intention of resisting if Hitler persisted in acts of aggression.

The government's indifference to the fate of Czechoslovakia and Poland seems to imply a lack of perception about the requirements of power balance politics in Europe. Indeed, the Chamberlain government did not think of power relations in that way. Convinced that the division of Europe into two armed camps had been crucial to the onset of the First World War, Chamberlain was determined to avoid another division, particularly one along ideological lines and, to that end, any appearance of building a phalanx against the dictators of central Europe. So potent was his determination that, combined with the low esteem for Poland and Czechoslovakia, it was virtually certain that those states would only serve as pawns in a larger game, not as valuable entities in themselves.[25] Whether that was more a reflection of ignorance about the realities of the European state system or a stubborn resolve to break with the ways of the past, it was another influential element in the movement toward appeasement.

This compendium of motive forces does not touch upon every element which played a role in the formulation of appeasement policy. Others emerge elsewhere in this book (see chapter 7). Some of the forces and factors which made for the policy still await detailed examination by historians; and it may well be, as Franklin Gannon wrote in 1971, that they are 'still too recent, too deeply felt, to be ready for detached reappraisal', especially since the appeasement of Nazi Germany was 'as much the result of a complex of attitudes and susceptibilities which divided the left and right in Britain, and split them within themselves, as it was the result of reaction to the Nazi regime'.[26] Hopefully, however, this summary demonstrates the breadth and complexity of the forces which stirred in Britain and gave appeasement appeal, however right or mistaken its pursuit is ultimately adjudged to have been.

---

[24] Gannon, *The British Press and Germany, 1936–1939*, pp. 19–20.
[25] Incongruous with the British estimate of Poland's military value and Chamberlain's sensitivity to Polish interests and wishes in dealing with Russia, this demonstrates the existence of some basic contradictions in Chamberlain's policies.
[26] Gannon, *The British Press and Germany, 1936–1939*, p. 31. See below, p. 98, n. 28.

5 Major Proponents of Appeasement

The idea of appeasement was compatible with a very broad range of British opinion in the 1930s. As Chamberlain strove initially to formulate and implement an active appeasement, particularly toward Germany and Italy, approval and goodwill characterized the reactions of an overwhelming majority of his countrymen who were aware, and alert to the implications, of his initiatives. In this sense, nearly all Englishmen were appeasers of sorts until the events of 1938 began to impel sharpening differences in policy appraisals. Even then distinctions between those who continued to support appeasement and those who came to oppose it are not always easily drawn. Many Englishmen experienced distressingly mixed emotions on the matter, their feelings subject to fluctuation with the course of events and the intermittent predominance of hope and disappointment. At the same time, there were those who, by virtue of position and influence, obviously were prime movers in appeasement and whose commitment to the policy was strong and enduring.

Laurence Lafore has put it succinctly and well: 'During the thirties, British policy was first influenced, and from early 1938 made, by a group of people who shared like opinions, listened to nobody who disagreed with them, and tried to replace or bypass the people in the government who did.' This group was 'definite in creed and power' but 'indefinite in composition'.[1]

In the early years of the historiography of appeasement much was attributed to the energizing force of 'the Cliveden set', an open-ended circle of well-educated, conservative-oriented, essentially aristocratic personalities, including government officials, who often gathered at Cliveden, the country home of Lord Astor, owner of *The Times*, to enjoy their own company and to share views on many matters of common interest. Since the conversations centred on public affairs and the sympathies of most Cliveden guests ran strongly in favour of appeasement, it was easy, especially for opponents, to assume that the policy sprang from this conspiratorial microcosm of Britain's ruling class. This thesis, however, has generally been discredited. However much support for

---

[1] Laurence Lafore, *The End of Glory: an Interpretation of the Origins of World War II* (Philadelphia, 1970), pp. 189–90. An appendix in Lammers, *Explaining Munich* (pp. 52–3), lists the most commonly named supporters of appeasement, as well as opponents, indicating their ages in 1938, education, and foreign office service or lack of it.

appeasement emanated from these gatherings, and however great the influence of participants in their various other contacts, there was clearly no cell, no conspiracy, no regular meetings, and no definite membership. Indeed, some of the most prominent appeasers rarely visited Cliveden. So while Cliveden discussions assuredly reinforced the direction in which British foreign policy was moving, and *The Times* became the foremost public organ of appeasement, efforts to identify and categorize the appeasers according to their Cliveden connections are clearly of limited value.

In similar fashion, there was once a widespread notion that the fellows of All Souls College, Oxford, formed a clique in which appeasement was conceived and nurtured—a notion of potential credibility inasmuch as a number of those fellows did become leading figures, both in government and outside it, associated with the promotion of appeasement. But A. L. Rowse, himself a fellow of All Souls, has destroyed that theory in one of the most penetrating, if polemical, treatises on appeasement, showing that 'the vast majority of us opposed it [appeasement]—some of us passionately—all the way along.'[2] So another effort to identify the appeasers in terms of an easily recognizable group of special affiliation is rendered useless.

Indeed, just as attempts to explain appeasement as some fixed and conscious objective determined by ideological or doctrinal prejudice have fallen short of the mark, attempts to identify the appeasers in terms of clear-cut ideological, social, educational or other groupings have proved inadequate. And, just as Chamberlain is best understood as a well-meaning, if sometimes stubborn, imprudent, and myopic man working within the complex and ambivalent characteristics of human society,[3] the leading proponents of appeasement are best identified as the prime minister and the ad hoc group of persons, deeply sympathetic to the policy, which he drew around him in order to advance it. Many of the leading appeasers had a number of traits in common, but it was the commitment to appeasement alone which constituted them as a group; everything else seems largely incidental.

It is difficult to single out special proponents of appeasement prior to 1937 because of the passive nature and wide general acceptance of the policy. But Neville Chamberlain himself was the guiding force in active appeasement. Without his energies the passivity of earlier years may have ended in something like the confusion, drift, and defeatism of French foreign policy in the latter 1930s. He was probably as vital to appeasement as Hitler was to Nazism. Born to a prominent political family,[4] he had entered business in Birmingham, attaining considerable

[2] A. L. Rowse, *Appeasement: a Study in Political Decline, 1933–1939* (New York, 1961), p. 108.

[3] See Rock, *Neville Chamberlain*, pp. 210–11.

[4] His father, Joseph Chamberlain, had held important cabinet posts and was a vigorous advocate of rapprochement with Germany at the turn of the century; his half-brother, Austen, became a foreign secretary in the 1920s.

stature among Midland industrialists and serving in various public capacities, including that of lord mayor, before his election to parliament in 1918. First entering the cabinet as postmaster general (1922), he later achieved an outstanding record as minister of health (1924–29) and served capably as chancellor of the exchequer (1931–37) during a time of severe economic stress. What he lacked in imagination and personal appeal he made up in efficiency, administrative skill, dedication, and a willingness to assume assignments shunned by other men. His interests and strengths lay largely in domestic politics (social, economic, health, and welfare problems); it is the irony of history that, as prime minister, he was preoccupied almost exclusively with foreign policy. He was certainly not ignorant of foreign affairs, as some have held, but he had no real 'touch' for a diplomatic situation, did not always grasp the full implications of foreign policy problems, and relied too heavily on his own judgement.

Chamberlain's commitment to appeasement is best explained in terms of two broad factors—his assessment of the European situation in 1937 and certain deep impulses or traits of his nature.[5] He was not simply a weak man propelled by fear or an appeaser 'by nature'. Indeed, he could be stern, obstinate, and uncompromising, quite intolerant and sometimes rude toward those who did not share his views. For instance, his relations with the Labour party and even the dissidents of his own party were thoroughly hostile, and he stubbornly refused to move from appeasement until long after its viability had been denied by all but its most die-hard defenders. More vital factors in his commitment to appeasement were his intense hatred of war, his belief in the basic reasonableness of all men, and his sense of personal mission to secure the peace of Europe. Convinced that 'the aim of every statesman worthy of the name, to whatever country he belongs, must be the happiness of the people for whom and to whom he is responsible',[6] the possibility that 'happiness', for some, might best be attained by means other than the maintenance of peace and quiet and order seemed to escape him. Chamberlain was not, it bears repeating, a theoretical pacifist, and as late as the middle 1930s had been a leader in limited rearmament. But he recoiled from the waste of war and deeply resented the sacrifice of British resources on the altar of military power when so many other human needs were pressing. There must be another way out of the tension which was building up in Europe. So he set out with determination, and abounding confidence in his own ability, to find it. It was as if fate had chosen him for this moment in history.

Closely associated with Chamberlain in appeasement were Lord Halifax, foreign secretary after February 1938, Sir Samuel Hoare, the home secretary, and Sir John Simon, chancellor of the exchequer.

---

[5] Theories of psychological instability, blind class prejudice, childlike ignorance and the like are at best misleading, at worst inaccurate.
[6] Chamberlain, *In Search of Peace*, p. 29. See above, p. 28.

Along with the prime minister they came to form, during the height of the Czech crisis, an 'inner cabinet' which met frequently and exercised strong influence in policy formulation. But their attachment to appeasement long preceded that critical moment; indeed, it was their general sympathy with Chamberlain's views, their sharing by instinct, training, and experience of his assumptions, aims, and methods, as well as their moderate, congenial temperaments, which first prompted their utilization as a small advisory body. And his apparent satisfaction with their advice and support led Chamberlain to continued reliance upon them in the anxious months thereafter.

Simon and Hoare were both former foreign secretaries, senior ministers with extensive experience and of recognized intellectual calibre. Both were cooperative, tractable men who fitted the requirement that nothing should be said or done which might offend the dictators. In their relations with Chamberlain, both tended toward sycophancy. That Simon had no special knowledge of national finance was immaterial to Chamberlain, who valued his advice on other matters. His indecisive nature was portrayed by a German embassy official as representative of 'that typically British mentality which prefers a bad compromise to a straight solution, if that solution involves the assumption of any responsibility'. And Lloyd George described him as having 'sat so long on the fence that the iron has entered his soul'.[7] Doubt that any other policy was possible strongly reinforced his conviction that appeasement was 'right'. Not until September 2nd, 1939, when he lost patience with Chamberlain's delay in declaring war, did he take real issue with the prime minister. Hoare was also a fervid appeaser, himself surmising that it was 'the sense of agreement both in outlook and method' which led Chamberlain to take him into his confidence on foreign affairs.[8] Indeed, their habits of life brought them continually together; the two men shared views daily during morning walks around the lake in St James's park. Cabinet records now available reveal Hoare, in 1939, as being less confident about appeasement than he had hitherto appeared, and pushing, after Prague, for the arranging of a tie with Russia in the interest of mutual defence. But his role as a leading supporter of Chamberlain's policy is not extensively altered.

Halifax is a somewhat different case. He served Chamberlain faithfully and well, obediently executing the policy set forth from above, deferring to his leader's initiatives, and providing, according to Chamberlain's own testimony, great comfort to his chief. Save for the week which preceded Munich, when he had his fill of Hitler's arrogant threats, he made little notable effort to influence Chamberlain's conduct of policy until March 1939. Thereafter, he showed relatively more initiative

[7] Gilbert and Gott, *The Appeasers*, p. 66.
[8] Templewood, *Nine Troubled Years*, pp. 257–8. Hoare writes extensively in his memoirs about foreign policy and his own involvement. Simon's memoirs are distressingly thin in this regard. See *Retrospect: the Memoirs of the Right Honourable Viscount Simon* (London, 1952).

and independence of thought, and progressively stronger interest in alternatives to appeasement.[9] Well before Prague, however, the construction he put on appeasement in both public and private was somehow different. He seemed more inclined to view it as unhappy necessity, not as positive good; more alert to its dangers and shortcomings; more willing to read the evidence on dictatorial behaviour for what it was than what he hoped it might be; more sensitive to the need for counter actions which would convey a sense of British strength and limits to her acquiescence in bullying. And his even temperament, bolstered by a character reputed as saintly, stood in sharp contrast to Chamberlain's frequently irascible manner. In consequence, Halifax often escaped the wrath of opponents, indeed to such a degree that he would have been an acceptable successor to Chamberlain in May 1940. He has also been treated more kindly by some historians of appeasement.[10]

Official advisers to the inner cabinet were Sir Alexander Cadogan, permanent under-secretary in the foreign office, and Sir Horace Wilson, special assistant to Chamberlain. Cadogan, whose position made him party to policy deliberations both in the foreign office and cabinet circles, was a cautious, conventional official sometimes caught up in a cross-fire between the two. Appointed to his post when Vansittart was removed for his anti-German bias by being 'elevated' to chief diplomatic advisor, Cadogan was generally inclined to accept the prime minister's views. But he also had his moments of doubt, when his judgement was offended by Nazi unreasonableness. Thus, for example, he rejected the Godesberg terms, favoured more vigorous rearmament, and encouraged, if vaguely, the arranging of closer relations with Britain's potential allies. His outlook is no doubt best described by his private secretary of that time: 'He was, at heart, always a revisionist rather than an appeaser.'[11] Cadogan's role related more to policy execution than formulation, but he was in a position to influence appeasement's form and direction, both subtly and openly.

Wilson is easier to categorize. Chamberlain's closest confident, his *eminence grise*, he was intimately involved in appeasement. Officially chief industrial adviser, and reputed to be a skilled administrator and negotiator, primarily in labour relations, he had been an unofficial counsellor in Downing Street since 1935, becoming involved only gradually in foreign affairs. Distrustful of the foreign office, Chamberlain installed Wilson in an office adjoining the cabinet room and gave him

[9] Lord Butler, then a foreign office official, testifies in his memoirs: 'I doubt whether sufficient credit has yet been given to Halifax for leading the cabinet swiftly but steadily in 1939 towards an inevitable declaration of war'. *The Art of the Possible*, p. 77.
[10] Halifax is the subject of a monumental biography by the earl of Birkenhead, *Halifax: the Life of Lord Halifax* (London, 1965). There is no full biography of Simon or Hoare.
[11] *The Memoirs of Lord Gladwyn* (New York, 1972), p. 82. Cadogan's views are generally apparent in David Dilks (editor), *The Diaries of Sir Alexander Cadogan, 1938–1945* (London, 1971).

wide-ranging unofficial duties in the conduct of foreign affairs, regularly seeking his counsel and using him as a personal emissary. Wilson, experienced, intelligent and respected, was thus a 'fluid person', free to operate as he and Chamberlain wished, responsible and loyal to Chamberlain alone. Naturally, the foreign office, though apparently not Halifax, resented this usurpation of its functions and the constant interference in its affairs. But Chamberlain believed the arrangement essential, and Wilson was the perfect man for the job.

The extent of Wilson's influence is difficult to measure. The basic ideas about appeasement were most assuredly Chamberlain's. But Wilson shared them, nurtured them, reinforced them, and lent to them the weight of his considerable reputation as a shrewd manipulator. And, serving so closely as Chamberlain's alter ego, his spokesman, and his emissary, he was able to interpret Chamberlain's views and to give them the inflection which particular occasions demanded. He was also much like Chamberlain in his dogged conviction that he possessed a superior understanding of the dictators and knew more about international relations than the diplomats.

In the pursuit of appeasement, then, Chamberlain relied heavily on the advice and support of Wilson and the inner cabinet. But neither had official status in the governmental hierarchy of foreign policy-making. The cabinet, and indirectly the foreign policy committee of the cabinet, did and Chamberlain had also to work with them.

Cabinet committees come and go as needs arise and disappear. The foreign policy committee came into being in April 1936, following the remilitarization of the Rhineland. It was partly Chamberlain's idea and suited his preference for a small inner group to formulate policy. A cluster of eight to eleven ministers, the number fluctuating according to the scope and weight of advice required on various occasions,[12] it met eleven times before Chamberlain became prime minister, lapsed for six months after mid-1937, reemerged in January 1938, met with some regularity until June, then lapsed again until mid-November. It was in this committee that much of the early brainstorming about appeasement, especially German colonial restitution, centred during 1936–37. Chamberlain was a leader in these discussions, by virtue of both personal interest and the influence of the treasury which he represented.[13] Up to late June 1937, when the committee adjourned for a time, seeing no immediate hope of appeasement, there was general approval if not enthusiasm for a policy of appeasement in a broad sense, not simply with respect to colonies, along with a frank recognition of

---

[12] Usually included were the prime minister, the foreign secretary, the lord president of the council, the lord chancellor, the ministers for war, the admiralty, and air, the minister of coordination of defence, the ministers for the dominions and colonies, the president of the board of trade, and sometimes the home secretary.

[13] His memorandum of April 1937 entitled 'Anglo-German Relations' was the basis of much discussion and reveals Chamberlain's thinking on appeasement at that time. See Colvin, *The Chamberlain Cabinet*, pp. 39–40.

some practical difficulties which would surely arise. When it reconvened in January 1938, Chamberlain was firmly established in leadership, his views and wishes were clear, and committee members were generally disposed to follow his lead—raising questions and expressing doubts about aspects of Chamberlain's outlook, but never resisting the prime minister when it came to the point of decision. In this way, all those who sat on the foreign policy committee were appeasers of some dimension. And this did not change materially up to the outbreak of war, partly because the prime minister often confronted the committee with decisions already taken, partly because he increasingly managed committee composition so as to include only those ministers known to be agreeable with the direction he proposed to take.

Much the same thing can be said of the full cabinet. Aside from Eden and Duff Cooper, who resigned, on separate occasions, in protest at Chamberlain's policy, and Lord Swinton, who was ousted from the air ministry (May 1938) for his stubborn insistence on expanded air strength, cabinet ministers approved Chamberlain's policy or accepted it without effective dissent. There were some younger men, disparagingly referred to by Chamberlain as the 'Boys' Brigade', who occasionally raised uncomfortable questions, levied token protests against appeasement, and once or twice even whispered revolt, but without voting their dissent or asking the secretary to record it.[14] A substantial majority, however, mostly senior ministers who had been in office for much of the past decade, was faithful and constant in support of their leader. In addition to members of the inner cabinet, this group included Sir Thomas Inskip (coordination of defence, later dominions), Lord Hailsham (lord chancellor, later lord president), Lord Zetland (India), Lord Stanhope (education), Lord Maugham (lord chancellor, after Hailsham), Lord Runciman (lord president, after Hailsham), Sir Kingsley Wood (air, after Swinton), Ernest Brown (labour), Sir John Anderson (lord privy seal), Lord Chatfield (coordination of defence, after Inskip), D. J. Colville (Scotland, after Elliot), and Leslie Burgin (transport, later minister without portfolio). Nor was Chamberlain ever willing to bring into the cabinet anyone with differing views on foreign affairs, though this was pressed upon him, notably after Munich and Prague, by Halifax and others. When changes occurred, the 'new' men were invariably 'old' men, most of whom possessed the requisite administrative ability, but brought no new or refreshing points of view to cabinet deliberations. So the cabinet continued as a primary collaborative agency to appeasement as long as peace prevailed.

In a still broader sense, most Conservative members of parliament (dissidents aside; see chapter 6) must be listed among the supporters

---

14 Middlemas, *Diplomacy of Illusion*, p. 316. This group included Eden, Oliver Stanley (board of trade), W. S. Morrison (agriculture), Walter Elliot (Scotland, later health), W. Ormsby-Gore (colonies), Malcolm MacDonald (dominions, then colonies), Leslie Hore-Belisha (war), Lord de la Warr (lord privy seal, later education), and Lord Winterton (chancellor of the Duchy of Lancaster).

of appeasement, though their support often seemed more like blind acquiescence than confident, active encouragement. Chamberlain commanded a majority of approximately 250 seats in the Commons, and all but 25 or 30 of the more than 350 Conservatives whom he inherited from Baldwin followed him unswervingly. This was due in part, no doubt, to British party discipline, Chamberlain's strong personal influence in the party organization,[15] and a natural reluctance among Conservatives to risk their political lives by contributing to a weakening of the Chamberlain government and the possible elevation of Labour to power. It also reflected a broad layer of sympathy with the foreign policy of the government and a general unconcern, and sometimes ignorance, about the procedural irregularities which appeared in Chamberlain's efforts to pursue it. Few of these 'regular' Conservative MPs ever spoke with conviction in the House of Commons. Month after month they listened to frequent debates on crucial foreign policy issues without the slightest murmur of doubt (except on March 16th and September 2nd, 1939) about the government's posture. Then, in divisions, they faithfully obeyed David Margesson, chief Conservative whip and advocate of appeasement, and regularly delivered the overwhelming majorities which Chamberlain sought, thus reinforcing his conviction in the rightness of his course. If misgivings about appeasement lingered beneath the surface, they remained submerged, unspoken and unvoted. No prime minister could have asked for more unquestioning allegiance, more docile concurrence.[16]

Within the foreign office feelings about appeasement were mixed and unsettled, and individuals difficult to classify with assurance. Among senior officials, opinion vacillated during the middle 1930s on the inevitability of war if Britain's vital interests were to be safeguarded, and the merits of deterrence, or containment, versus appeasement as the best means of dealing with Germany and Italy. Three different, if nebulous, groupings at length emerged—those who favoured containment, those who would keep the dictators guessing, and those who leaned toward appeasement, or at least rejected the indefinite postponement of efforts at reconciliation with Germany and Italy. Cadogan and William Strang, head of the central department, were associated with the latter group, Cadogan somewhat irregularly, Strang increasingly so as 1938 wore on. Among other notable adherents to the third point of view were a trio of ambassadors, Sir Nevile Henderson (Berlin), Lord Perth (Rome), and Lord Chilston (Moscow, until late

---

[15] His work as party chairman in 1930–31, his influence as chancellor of the exchequer with contributors to Conservative campaign funds, and his service as Baldwin's agent in various party activities all made for a party organization sensitive to his touch. Indeed, in the election of 1935 many Conservative candidates were personally familiar with and temperamentally sympathetic to him.

[16] For all practical purposes, the government was an oligarchy in which Chamberlain functioned almost dictatorially. See Marion L. Kenney, 'The Role of the House of Commons in British Foreign Policy during the 1937–38 Session', in Norton Downs (editor), *Essays in Honor of Conyers Read* (Chicago, 1953), pp. 144, 180–85.

1938), and the minister in Prague, Basil Newton. During 1938 they were joined by Sir Eric Phipps (ambassador in Berlin to early 1937, thereafter in Paris), whose earlier association with the containment group was gradually eroded by his own gloomy assessment of French morale. These men originated the bulk of advice received in London from the capitals of Europe most closely concerned with Czechoslovakia in 1938.[17]

None of these diplomats had attained his post because of his views on appeasement; all of them came around to supporting the policy, on varying bases, as a result of their observations and experiences 'on the job.' Perth, who had been in Rome since 1933, was convinced during 1937–38 that British initiative in reaching a sympathetic understanding of Italian interests could restore Anglo-Italian relations at least to what they had been before the Abyssinian episode. Newton was impressed, critics might say obsessed, with the view that Czechoslovakia was a hybrid creation whose capacity for survival was doubtful; military action in defence of her existing form would be futile since she could not survive even a victorious campaign. Henderson saw his work in Berlin as a mission—to believe in German honour and good sense, and thus to soothe Anglo-German relations, on which the peace of Europe depended. All were influential, especially since their views corresponded with Chamberlain's. Henderson was particularly so, and is worthy of special mention.

A career diplomat who had served capably in Belgrade and Buenos Aires, Henderson was assigned to Berlin early in 1937 by the foreign secretary, Anthony Eden, on the strong recommendation of Robert Vansittart. The irony of this is great in view of their intense differences, later on, over the appeasement of Germany. He seemed the best available man, and no one in the foreign office foresaw the opinions he was later to hold.[18] Henderson undertook his new assignment feeling 'specially selected by Providence with the definite mission of. . . helping to preserve the peace of the world'.[19] And his sense of predestination grew in proportion to the difficulties he encountered. He openly sympathized with the Nazis, proclaimed their good intentions, made excuses for them, supported their claims in Austria and Czechoslovakia, thus perhaps helping to accelerate events, and habitually interpreted instructions from the foreign office in a manner friendlier to Germany than what was in fact intended. His reports and dispatches, carefully studied by Chamberlain and the cabinet, regularly reinforced Chamberlain's own ideas, hopes, and convictions. His advice was sometimes crucial, as in the abandoning of a strongly-worded warning to Hitler in the early days of September 1938, and the promotion of a

---

[17] Middlemas, *Diplomacy of Illusion*, pp. 70–72.
[18] Earl of Avon, *The Memoirs of Anthony Eden: Facing the Dictators* (London and Boston, 1962), p. 570.
[19] Sir Nevile Henderson, *Failure of a Mission: Berlin, 1937–1939* (New York, 1940), pp. 3–4.

virtual campaign to talk peace and confidence into being through public pronouncements of excessive optimism during the first two months of 1939. It was not that Henderson failed entirely to perceive the ills and dangers in Nazi policies and actions, or even sometimes to be greatly annoyed by them. Rather, he simply refused to interpret portents and events to mean what he did not want them to mean.

Appeasement had some powerful supporters outside official government circles. Pre-eminent among them was Geoffrey Dawson, editor of *The Times*. Intimate with Chamberlain, as few persons were, as well as his Yorkshire neighbour Halifax, Dawson was primarily concerned with the safety and vitality of the British Empire and inclined to feel no great clash of interest with Germany on the continent. He shared the view that German grievances were legitimate, and that justice did not become injustice because it was a dictator who demanded it. An affinity for Germany underscored his conviction that Britain should 'explore every avenue' in search of a reasonable understanding with her. He performed his editing duties with an eye to including items which would soothe the Germans and excluding things which would 'hurt their susceptibilities'.[20] His position gave him unique advantages of access to men and offices, a constant awareness of the prime minister's thinking, numerous chances to express his own opinions on foreign policy, and occasional opportunities to float trial balloons, as in the famous leader of September 7th, 1938, advocating the transfer of the Sudetenland from Czechoslovakia to Germany. Whether his influence amounted to more than a powerful reinforcement of Chamberlain's natural inclinations, as Chamberlain's convictions reinforced his own, is hard to say. But that role was immense, reflected as it was in the pages of *The Times*, the most influential newspaper in Britain, read and respected by nearly everyone concerned with the making of British foreign policy.[21]

The Times had no foreign editor, so responsibility for foreign affairs rested with Dawson. His contacts were wide, his schedule full of meetings with people knowledgable about the European situation. One of those on whom he relied in German matters was Lord Lothian, Philip Kerr, a highly respected Liberal intellectual with experience in government, wide-ranging contacts, and a reputation for fairness, moral uprightness, and balanced judgement. Indeed, Lothian is important to this account not simply in his own right, but as a representative type of person—of whom there were many, including some prominent intellectuals—who believed in appeasement, promoted its acceptance, and, by virtue of

---

[20] Gilbert, *The Roots of Appeasement*, pp. 143–4.
[21] *The Times* was widely regarded as an official mouthpiece for the government. The chief leader writer was deputy editor Robert Barrington-Ward, who along with Dawson, made *The Times* a more thorough and consistent supporter of appeasement than any other newspaper. On Dawson and *The Times*, see John Evelyn Wrench, *Geoffrey Dawson and Our Times* (London, 1955); *The History of The Times* IV, part 2 (New York, 1952); and Gannon, *The British Press and Germany, 1936–1939*.

personal reputation and friendship with figures in high places, made his influence felt.

Lothian had twice made 'the visit to Hitler'[22] in 1935 and 1937, and had come away confirmed in his belief that appeasement was a feasible policy. Hitler did not want war; he was profoundly pre-occupied with Russia and the communist danger; and he regarded Anglo-German cooperation as essential to the stability of Europe. His muted claims for political rearrangement in central Europe were not unreasonable and would not adversely affect Britain's vital interests on the continent. Nazi brutality, especially in the form of antisemitism, was certainly disturbing; but it was 'largely the reflex of external per-secution' to which the Germans themselves had been subjected since the war.[23] For Britain to join the 'old encirclement group' would simply mean war again. Only appeasement was sensible and moral.

Though Lothian later, in 1938, recognized the errors in his assessment of German aims, for a few years he had spread his views with diligence and conviction. His country house at Blickling rivalled Cliveden as a gathering place for notables of all kinds to socialize and discuss politics. He made frequent addresses, particularly at the Royal Institute of Inter-national Affairs (Chatham House) and in the House of Lords, and often wrote letters to *The Times*, where they were welcomed and utilized. He corresponded with a growing circle of prominent supporters, and some sceptics as well, and generally promoted appeasement as effectively as it was possible to do in the role of private citizen.

Of comparable influence, though of a somewhat different kind, was Thomas Jones, private secretary to Baldwin and a close friend of the Astors, Dawson, and Lothian. A Germanophile by training and instinct, positively appreciative of some aspects of the Nazi regime, and con-vinced, partly by Arnold Toynbee, of Hitler's sincerity in desiring peace in Europe and friendship with Britain, he too had made the visit to Hitler in 1936. Thoroughly reassured, he vainly encouraged Baldwin to do the same. As a central figure in the Cliveden group and one who moved constantly in political circles, he maintained connections with many of the leading proponents of appeasement, both inside and outside the government, sharing the views of one with another and interposing his own opinions along the way. Like Lothian, he became disillusioned with appeasement before 1938 was out, and, like Lothian, he warrants identification here not as an exceptional advocate of appeasement, but because he is broadly representative of the highly placed 'unofficial' Englishman who lent strong support to the policy for a time.[24]

[22] Gilbert and Gott show that a personal meeting with Hitler was near-ritualistic among leading 'independent' appeasers who wished to discover the prospects of dealing with the Führer directly. *The Appeasers*, pp. 49ff.

[23] J. R. M. Butler, *Lord Lothian* (London, 1960), p. 206. This book contains many letters to and from a prominent appeaser.

[24] Thomas Jones, *A Diary with Letters, 1931–1950* (London, 1954), is very revealing on appeasement and appeasers.

Further enumeration of such persons would be at best incomplete and perhaps unfairly selective. Suffice it to say there were many; and their presence throughout the ranks of English society, and especially in the upper strata, provided a backdrop against which Chamberlain could move ahead with confidence insofar as support at home was concerned. Their broad perception of the international situation in the latter half of the 1930s may now be summarized.

There was a certain logic in active appeasement which provided the policy with much of its force.[25] With Germany menacing in central Europe, Italy rampaging in Spain and Ethiopia, and Japan conducting a campaign of aggression in mainland China, the peace of the world was tottering. Moreover, these three militarist powers, having withdrawn from the League of Nations, or in the case of Italy, on the verge of withdrawal, were linking together in an international front of yet unknown but potentially dangerous proportions. Could nothing be done to combat this trend, reverse it, and thus preserve the peace, at least in Europe?

Of the possible methods by which the peace of Europe might be maintained, appeasement seemed to offer the best prospect of success. Collective security through the League of Nations had failed abjectly in several previous tests. Small states were inevitably reluctant to take any initiative in operations against powerful aggressors, so the burden would fall on a sharply limited number of large powers, essentially Britain and France, if the League could agree to act at all. Besides, the principle of collective security was rapidly becoming a divisive issue in British party politics. The Conservatives in power increasingly resented the Labour party's badgering about their betrayal of the principle, while Labour adamantly refused to support even a modest military establishment by which Britain could realistically contribute to European collective security. Indeed, the very term 'collective security' came to be regarded by many leading Conservatives as a meaningless shibboleth of partisan politics, which spurred their resistance to it.

A vigorous pursuit of alliance arrangements with other powers opposed to the Rome-Berlin Axis was another possibility. But that did not appeal to the proponents of appeasement theoretically or realistically. The alliance system which preceded the First World War had significantly reduced the diplomatic flexibility of individual powers, made it virtually impossible to evaluate specific problems on their own merits, transformed lesser disputes into crises of European dimensions, and thus promoted the atmosphere of suspicion and tension which led to war. Surely it was unwise to resort to such a scheme again. Moreover, who would join Britain in such a system? Not the United States, and not Russia, who might join but could not be trusted. That left France, whose fidgety obsession with her own security had already spoiled

[25] This discussion draws heavily on Charles L. Mowat, *Britain between the Wars, 1918—1940* (Chicago, 1955; London, 1968), pp. 509ff.

Versailles and perverted the purposes of the League, whose military strength did not match its inflated reputation, and whose Popular Front government hardly inspired confidence among business and conservative circles in Britain. Appeasement of the dictators certainly seemed preferable.

There was, of course, a possibility that the dictators were not appeasable. The vicious, unpredictable element in Hitler's behaviour, as well as the pompous, fickle nature of Mussolini, were already quite apparent. And the evils of fascist, particularly Nazi, tyranny did not appear substantially different from those of communist tyranny, with which no compromise was considered possible. But whereas the evils of communism, gestating for a half century or more, seemed eternal, the evils of Nazism, which appeared with surprising suddenness, and with little ideological foundation, might be 'killed by kindness'. Quite possibly Hitler was only a shrewd politician, a worthy heir to Bismarck and Stresemann, taking calculated risks, but knowing when to stop. Furthermore, the German people, the ones who really mattered, were basically reasonable, wise, and stable, more compatible with Englishmen in temperament and aspirations than Frenchmen or Slavs. So an Anglo-German agreement would prove as trustworthy as any agreement between several sovereign nations. Such was the logic of appeasement, 'defended with the fanaticism of a faith'.[26]

If it should develop that Hitler would not keep his word, that he would not be satisfied with equality of status, that his ultimate objectives directly endangered European peace and security, the proponents of appeasement relied on the reinsurance policy embodied, they believed, in the programme of British rearmament. They did not think and speak of appeasement alone. Rather, they consistently espoused a double line—appeasement and rearmament.[27]

A double policy invariably requires skilful handling. The maintenance of a balance is often difficult, requiring a quick and delicate touch as well as constant effort on several fronts. Chamberlain and his colleagues increasingly gave the impression that they were leaning much more heavily to one side than the other. But they did not see it that way. The rearmament programme reluctantly initiated in 1934 had yet to produce substantial results in first-line strength; but it gave promise of a system of defence sufficient to provide a formidable deterrent to any aggressor and capable of ensuring a decisive victory in the air once British production overcame the German lead. And they were inclined to rely on promise. Further, the bitter opposition of the Labour party tended to leave the proponents of appeasement convinced that it was impossible to advance rearmament with greater speed. Undismayed by this, they persisted in the belief that Britain could react effectively

---

[26] Gilbert and Gott, *The Appeasers*, p. 47; Gilbert, *The Roots of Appeasement*, p. 143.
[27] In his memoirs, Sir Samuel Hoare (Lord Templewood), devotes a chapter to 'The Double Line'. *Nine Troubled Years*, pp. 283–90.

should the force of circumstances absolutely require a military response. There was much more question in their minds about the national will and the psychological rallying power of the British people behind a military effort than about the ultimate military capability of the nation. The slowness of British rearmament notwithstanding, the proponents of appeasement were not much motivated by the need to buy time until the nation's military preparedness was significantly improved. Even the later defence of Munich on these grounds appeared only after the event itself, and was not embraced by leading appeasers at the time. Rather, the appeasers' commitment to their policy grew out of a belief that it would 'work', or at least that its chances of working were good enough to warrant giving it every opportunity. The manner and method of Munich raised serious doubts in the minds of some; and the German occupation of Prague rudely convulsed the confidence of many others. But some of them even then, and Chamberlain in particular, were not yet fully convinced that the policy had finally failed. So it lingered on, largely in abeyance, subject to Hitler's mercy.

6 Major Opponents of Appeasement

Much the same thing can be said about the major opponents of appeasement as was noted about its major supporters: distinctions are not always easily drawn, and many of those who came to oppose the policy did so only gradually and sometimes fitfully. Even Winston Churchill, widely regarded by popular opinion as the 'original' anti-appeaser, occupied, up to the Austrian *Anschluss*, a position more ambiguous than is generally assumed.[1] What separated Chamberlain from his gradually multiplying opponents, as 1938–39 unfolded, was not so much a fundamental disagreement over the validity of appeasement as a legitimate technique of foreign policy, but intensifying differences as to whether the circumstances were then 'right' for its implementation, whether its primary objects, Hitler and Mussolini, were in fact appeasable, whether Chamberlain's methods and timing were appropriate and, most importantly, whether the policy was succeeding or failing.

While reservations about appeasement based on principle or partisan politics existed in a few quarters before 1938, it was the circumstances and issues relating to Anthony Eden's resignation as foreign secretary in late February 1938, which provided the first occasion for open debate in which critics began to express their views.[2] The government's apparent willingness to succumb to Italy's 'now or never' attitude toward Anglo-Italian negotiations and to make significant concessions to Italy, including recognition of her Abyssinian conquest, in order to strike a deal with her, raised questions of international morality and political judgement which prompted an eruption of criticism, mainly but not entirely along predictable party lines, in sections of parliament and the press. And this was at a time when the Italians were openly flaunting bad faith in international dealings by supporting the Nationalist side in the Spanish Civil War in direct violation of the non-intervention agreement. For Eden himself, the prime minister's actions in rejecting Roosevelt's initiative of mid-January were also important, but the president's proposal was a well kept secret at the time. The shock of the Austrian *Anschluss* several weeks later lent support

[1] See p. 76. One of the most consistent, outspoken, early anti-appeasers was Sir Horace Rumbold, ambassador in Berlin, 1928–33.
[2] Eden's under-secretary, Viscount Cranborne, also resigned in protest against the government's policy.

to those who had now begun to question the wisdom of attempting to appease unscrupulous dictators; and the two events, taken together, constituted the first important challenge to appeasement.

As trouble brewed in Czechoslovakia, opponents of appeasement counselled firmly against any solution reached by force or the threat of force. Their suggested methods diverged in several directions. A majority of the critics stood for a firm British role in upholding international obligations and resisting aggression, some of them prepared to countenance military means if necessary, others inclined to rely on the moral force still thought to reside in the League of Nations. A minority, especially those who looked to the Empire as Britain's source of strength, favoured a policy of British non-involvement. Munich was viewed as a national humiliation, resulting in sharply increased danger and settling nothing. Amid the wave of emotional relief which swept the nation, warning voices were in fact raised. There was wide acknowledgment in the press that, however commendable Chamberlain's efforts, Munich was a 'diktat' causing grave concern for the future. Debate in the House of Commons (October 3rd–6th), in which speakers from all parties called attention to the terrible price which had been paid for peace, was instrumental in returning the nation to its senses. As it began to dawn on them how curious it was that Munich was received with much more enthusiasm by the 'losers' in London and Paris than by the 'winners' in Berlin, the very shock of their own relief set more Englishmen to hard thinking. The cruel concessions made in the name of expediency began to bother more consciences; and there developed a perceptible undercurrent of disquieted feeling that perhaps Britain should have stood and fought, had Hitler persisted in his foolish threats. Accordingly, appeasement's critics grew in number, and those who spoke out gained greater credence.

The period from Munich to Prague was one of mixed and suspended judgement as the government worked to combine a policy of more earnest rearmament with continuing devotion to appeasement. Warning voices persisted, but hope for the best remained dominant. With the German attack on Prague the British instinct for self-preservation, disturbed by the turn of events at Munich, was thoroughly aroused and newly augmented by wounded pride. Hitler had lied and cheated! He could not be trusted. He must now be stopped.

The resulting clamour in parliament and press, and among the public generally, for a new and vigorous policy to meet the Nazi menace had much to do with the apparent revolution in British policy which followed. Denunciation of appeasement reached such suddenly expanded proportions, and persisted with such intensity, that failure to respond to it might well have meant the end of the Chamberlain government. The guarantee to Poland followed, after two weeks of frantic, and unsuccessful, diplomatic manoeuvring toward other less drastic options, and then guarantees to Greece and Rumania and negotiations with Russia looking toward her inclusion in a European bloc which could prevent further aggression. Meanwhile, the outcry against further appeasement abated only a little and was reinforced by a surprisingly broad anxiety to conclude a pact with Russia and growing impatience with the government's failure to do so. And so it remained up to the eve of war.[3]

Among the primary opponents of appeasement was the Labour party, which disagreed with the National government (no longer national after 1932) on almost every issue of foreign policy during the 1930s. It did not always present a united front, for the Labour movement was seriously divided within its own ranks on a number of issues. Consensus did at length emerge, however, on support for a policy of collective security through the League of Nations. That was not as simple as it sounded, for the party vehemently opposed national rearmament, and thus occupied the ambiguous position of embracing a policy which implied the potential use of armaments while refusing to support or sanction measures which would have provided them. But Labourites were generally satisfied with their own distinctions—opposition to purely national armaments though not to a British contribution toward the armed forces of the League, and steady opposition to the service estimates as a customary means of contesting the level of armaments or some other policy of the government but not necessarily all armaments[4]; and the contradiction in their outlook never seriously hampered their criticism of appeasement in their own eyes, though it certainly compromised their effectiveness in the eyes of others.

Since support for the League of Nations and collective security was fundamental in the electoral campaign of November 1935, which brought the Baldwin government into power, general agreement on foreign policy seemed possible. But appeasement, as Chamberlain formulated it, rejected collective action in favour of personal, individual, approaches to the dictators, while bluntly denying the League's ability to function effectively in solving Europe's problems and maintaining peace. Consequently, Labour's castigation of appeasement came regularly to incorporate the charge of base and devious reversal in the foreign policy platform on which the government had been elected.

Partisan political motives notwithstanding, Labour's perception of the possibility of safe and successful negotiation with the dictators proved to be much more accurate than the government's. From Eden's resignation onward, Labour leaders consistently warned that the dictators could not be trusted; that 'crawling before them' was a dangerous

---

[3] The foregoing paragraphs draw heavily on Rock, *Appeasement on Trial.*
[4] See Clement Attlee, *As It Happened* (New York 1954), pp. 138–9. In his memoirs, Attlee terms the latter practice 'old fashioned' and 'perhaps unwise and pedantic'. Hugh Dalton, another leading Labourite, agrees. *The Fateful Years: Memoirs, 1931–1945* (London, 1957), p. 175.

gamble that would surely result in the loss of respect, honour, and friends; that firmness was the essence of statesmanship and that appeasement was 'spineless nonsense'. This critical view was advanced on dozens of occasions in the House of Commons, in the context of every debate on foreign affairs and in response to the crucial episodes with which the years 1938–39 were so liberally dotted.[5]

Labour was passionately opposed to dealing with Mussolini in view of his clearly deceitful role in Spain. Its opposition sprang both from a broad regard for international morality and sympathy for the Republican cause in the Spanish conflict. Alarmed by the *Anschluss* and still more by Chamberlain's lenitive reaction to it, party spokesmen called for the replacement of bargains with dictators by a firm stand on the rule of law through the League. Britain must begin organizing a peace front of all countries outside the Rome–Berlin Axis. Throughout the developing Czechoslovak crisis Labour stood for 'firmness', asserting that every fresh concession, instead of advancing appeasement, only made the aggressors more openly arrogant and insolent. Grudging approval was granted to Chamberlain's September visits to Germany, but mainly in the hope that he might finally and firmly 'set the Führer straight'. Condemning Munich as abject surrender, Labour sponsored a parliamentary motion of disapproval of the government's conduct of foreign affairs, demanded a 'real peace conference' to deal with the potential causes of war, and reiterated the call for a bloc of states to resist aggression. Chamberlain was likened to a Samaritan taking the clothes off the wayfarer and giving them to the robber. The government's ambition to be eaten last was futile, for left alone, Britain would be eaten all the same and would not be consulted about the date of the banquet. Chamberlain's visit to Rome evoked strong protests against 'further surrender' and prompted comparisons to the well known nursery rhyme about the spider and the fly. In the aftermath of Prague, Labour intensified the demand for a broad anti-aggression bloc, approving the guarantee to Poland as the nucleus for such an arrangement, to be characterized by clearly defined obligations on the understanding that an attack against one was an attack upon all. It pressed relentlessly for an arrangement with the Soviet Union and constantly castigated Chamberlain's failure to achieve it. As the German threat hovered over Poland, Labour spokesmen insisted that the British guarantee must be honoured in full. And when Chamberlain faltered in declaring war on Germany for her invasion of Poland, it was left to a Labour leader, Greenwood, summoned from across the House of Commons by a distraught Conservative to 'speak for England', to express the resolve of the British nation.

[5] There were twenty-four important debates on foreign policy during the parliamentary session, February–July, 1938. In addition, the government had to answer 1400 questions on foreign affairs during the same period. See *House of Commons Debates*, July 26th, 1938, col. 3033 Nor did the pace slacken after Munich. Interest and anxiety were obvious, and on most of these occasions Labour criticism was in the forefront.

Labour leadership in the House of Commons was entrusted to Clement Attlee and Arthur Greenwood, one of whom always denounced appeasement when foreign policy issues were up for discussion. But at least thirty other Labour MPs participated at one time or another in presenting the Labour view. Prominent among them, both in frequency of speaking and sharpness of criticism, were Hugh Dalton and Josiah Wedgwood, followed by Herbert Morrison, Stafford Cripps,[6] P. J. Noel-Baker, F. J. Bellenger, and Ellen Wilkinson. These and many other Labourites also addressed public gatherings of all kinds on foreign policy matters, their views thus appearing regularly in the press. Among British newspapers, the mass-circulation *Daily Herald* was the chief organ of Labour views, while the prominent *New Statesman and Nation*, was a leading periodical reflecting the Labour outlook. Labour had, in consequence, no difficulty airing its perspective in various forums; the problem lay in achieving a broader acceptance of its view.

Indeed, the Labour impact on government policy was slight. Before March 1939, its suggested alternative to appeasement was regarded by the government as vague and meaningless, clearly outdated, and wholly out of touch with the needs of the times. After Prague, Labour pointed specifically towards an objective, an alliance with Russia, which the government was prepared to consider only as a last resort. So Labour's thundering and needling on foreign affairs, poised against a broad background of basic disagreement on domestic issues as well, evoked little or no response, save irritation and impatience, from the government side.

The foreign policy outlook of the declining Liberal party in the 1930s was similar to that of Labour. Since Versailles, Liberals had advocated the maintenance of peace by means of collective security, general disarmament but the retention of 'sufficient' defence forces, and the use by the League of Nations of sanctions, economic or military, against any nation defying its authority and engaging in aggression. To the Baldwin–Chamberlain policy the Liberal party was in almost continuous opposition. It disapproved the cold-shouldering of Russia, condemned the desertion of the League over Abyssinia and the pusillanimous toleration of German and Italian intervention in Spain and, after the course of events had compelled a fundamental change of position on military preparedness, began to criticize the inadequate effort towards Britain's rearmament. On the latter issue the Liberal party was quicker than the Labour party to recognize changing reality. In consequence, the Liberals dissociated themselves from Labour on that issue in 1936. But broad agreement on other matters continued, and their common opposition to appeasement brought them together

---

[6] Cripps was something of a maverick, who was expelled from the party in January 1939, for issuing a memorandum on cooperation with other anti-government groups, to which the party leadership objected. But this did not adversely affect his opposition to appeasement. See p. 79, n. 23.

on nearly all foreign policy matters debated in the House of Commons after 1937.[7]

Sir Archibald Sinclair, leader of the party, followed Attlee or Greenwood in Commons debates, and his posture on specific issues regularly coincided with Labour's, reinforcing it and sometimes sharpening it. He constantly decried Britain's retreat before the bluff and bluster of the dictators. After the *Anschluss*, he pressed the case for rallying peace-loving powers in a system of mutual assistance. Lamenting the fact that Britain was always restraining the victims of aggression, he asserted that appeasement could only result in war, when Britain's turn to be attacked at length arrived, or in craven surrender. Rejecting Munich as a victory for negotiation over force, he appealed for Britain to 'grapple her friends to her' (France, Russia, the United States, Holland, Belgium, and Switzerland) and offer 'convincing proof' to Germany that nations favouring law and reason in international relationships were prepared to work together in resisting force. Exasperated by the British recognition of Francoist Spain in February 1939, he offered a fitting epitaph for the Chamberlain government: 'We have eaten dirt in vain.' Prague prompted Sinclair again to denounce appeasement as 'disastrously misconceived', to add Rumania, Turkey, and some Balkan states to the list of nations which Britain must rally to form a bloc against aggression, and to conclude that only staff conversations for common military action would now suffice. The Liberals' opposition to conscription, primarily in deference to long-standing principle, survived even in late April 1939, and constituted a highly distracting element in the otherwise steady Liberal demand for a tougher foreign policy. But Sinclair and the party impatiently pressed for a quick and inclusive agreement with Russia; and the German threat to Danzig was matched by Liberal determination that Britain must stand firm, not merely for security but for the moral values of civilized life.[8]

Sinclair was not the only spokesman for the Liberal viewpoint. David Lloyd George, the former prime minister (1916–22), though earlier enthusiastic about Hitler's work in Germany,[9] was always in the thick of the controversy, the weight of his influence resting uneasily between his long experience and reputation as a practical politician on one hand, and the unkind suspicion of approaching senility, or at least destructive partisanship, on the other. No one used more colourful language to attack and discredit appeasement, and many major debates on foreign affairs were punctuated and enlivened by references to the prime minister's dovelike innocence rendering him fit only for a stained glass window, his magnificent skill in sprinting away from his obliga-

---

[7] See Viscount Samuel, *Memoirs* (London, 1945), pp. 269ff.

[8] Sinclair's, and the Liberal party's, position on various foreign policy issues during 1938–39 is traced in Rock, *Appeasement on Trial*.

[9] He had made a visit to Hitler in September 1936, and found him a born leader, a dynamic personality of high quality.

tions at Munich, his constant clucking to the dictators like an old hen trying to cross a busy road, and his inexcusable snobbery in looking a gift horse, Russia, in the mouth. Geoffrey Mander, Wilfred Roberts, Richard Acland and other Liberals occasionally added pointed objections to particular aspects of appeasement.

In the press, the mass-circulation *News Chronicle* was perhaps the leading vessel of official Liberal policy; but the influential *Manchester Guardian*, especially well informed on foreign affairs, was of great importance in reflecting Liberal views in the context of its independent orientation. It had a clear and accurate conception of Nazi Germany, and while it did not always draw the logical conclusions of its insight, it consistently noted the dangers of appeasement and sometimes firmly condemned it.[10] The *Economist* was a leading periodical in which Liberal views on appeasement found forceful expression, while the *Liverpool Daily Post* and the *Yorkshire Observer* were notable Liberal organs among provincial dailies. Like Labour, the Liberal opposition to appeasement did not lack regular and competent expression. But since the party's numbers were small and its threat to the government weak, its admonitions went largely unheeded.

Among the keenest critics of appeasement were a small number of dissident Conservatives, stronger in quality than in quantity, who came to believe that concessions to the dictators only whetted their appetites. Consequently, Britain, in close cooperation with France, must stand firm against escalating dictatorial demands, and be prepared to resist aggression by force of arms by coming to the aid of other victims without waiting until she herself was directly attacked. In a study of Conservative opposition to appeasement, Neville Thompson observes 'a picture of sporadic and discontinuous dissent, of individual critics and small cliques but no cohesive group'.[11] It was difficult to criticize a government controlled by one's own party, which commanded an overwhelming majority of loyal adherents, and whose policy seemed in harmony with widely accepted ideas. And the problems of devising sound alternatives, producing leaders, cooperating with Labour and the Liberals, and resisting Conservative party pressure to conform were formidable ones indeed. So few Conservative critics opposed the government constantly or confidently, particularly before Munich; and a carefully planned, agreed-upon alternative to appeasement did not in fact emerge. Nevertheless, there were thoughtful, respected Conservatives who were deeply troubled by the deteriorating international situation and the Chamberlain government's response to it; and their persistent doubting and questioning were instrumental both in opening and enlarging public debate about appeasement and in promoting an

[10] On the *Manchester Guardian*, see Gannon, *The British Press and Germany, 1936–1939*, pp. 74–88 and *passim*.
[11] Neville Thompson, *The Anti-Appeasers: Conservative Opposition to Appeasement in the 1930s* (Oxford, 1971), p. 2.

intensive soul-searching which helped to precondition the finality with which appeasement was ultimately abandoned by the English people.

In the forefront among the Conservative critics of appeasement were Anthony Eden and Winston Churchill. Eden became the central figure in a small group of dissident Conservatives which supported traditional diplomacy and the balance of power to a greater extent than the cabinet and opposed concessions to Germany and Italy without substantial guarantees for the future. This 'Eden Group', or 'the Glamour Boys', as they were scornfully labelled by the government whips, was an open, informal discussion group without fixed membership or policy positions. It comprised about twenty MPs, predominantly younger men, and included Lord Cranborne, L. S. Amery, Richard Law, Edward Spears, Harold Macmillan, Harold Nicolson (a National Labour MP and a vocal critic of appeasement), Sir Derrick Gunston, and Anthony Crossley. Churchill, who stood somewhat apart from the Eden group, partly by his own choosing, partly by theirs, had a few close followers, including Brendan Bracken, Robert Boothby, and Sir Roger Keyes. There was basic empathy on foreign policy issues between the two groups and fairly regular contact, especially as the Czech crisis climaxed. Eden and Churchill consulted frequently; Duncan Sandys and Harold Macmillan acted as informal liaisons between the groups.[12]

Eden's resignation as foreign secretary in February 1938 over differences with Chamberlain of both policy, particularly toward Italy,[13] and method, made him one of the earliest Conservative critics of consequence. His address of resignation emphasized the dangers of succumbing to intimidation, of neglecting sound and time-honoured principles of international conduct. Effective diplomacy was nearly always a matter of give-and-take; he would not consent to negotiations in which one side alone was expected to do all the giving. Rather, this was the time and place for Britain to stand firm.[14] Eden did not, however, assume thereafter the role of a crusader against appeasement. Content with warnings and admonitions, he did not devote his prestige and influence to the tasks of organizing opposition to Chamberlain's policy or posing a clear alternative to it. Wise, perhaps, in terms of party loyalty and future political ambitions, his cautious posture no doubt

---

[12] Thompson, *The Anti-Appeasers*, pp. 167–70; Earl of Avon, *The Memoirs of Anthony Eden: the Reckoning* (London and Boston, 1965), pp. 31–2; Harold Macmillan, *Winds of Change, 1914–1939* (London and New York, 1966), pp. 495–6. Others in the Eden group included J. P. L. Thomas, Mark Patrick, Paul Emrys-Evans, Viscount Wolmer, Ronald Tree, Sir Sidney Herbert, Hubert Duggan, Robert Bower, Dudley Joel, Ronald Cartland, C. G. Lancaster, and Duncan Sandys.

[13] Eden's policy differences with Chamberlain pertained mainly to Italy, not necessarily to Germany. See Colvin, *The Chamberlain Cabinet*, pp. 97–8; Northedge, *The Troubled Giant*, p. 488.

[14] *House of Commons Debates*, February 21st, 1938, col. 45–50.

reduced the potential impact of his opposition and the chances of forcing a change in British policy.[15]

Churchill was less reserved in his criticism and more specific in offering alternatives. While he was not an adamant opponent of appeasement before 1938[16], partly, no doubt, because its ultimate form and direction were still uncharted, the circumstances of Eden's resignation deeply disturbed him, and that, along with the shock of the Austrian *Anschluss*, prompted his swift emergence as an outspoken critic of what he now believed to be the sheer inadequacy of government policy. In the House of Commons on March 14th, he urged the construction of a 'grand alliance'—a number of states assembled around Britain and France in a solemn treaty for mutual protection, their forces marshalled in a common endeavour, their staff arrangements concerted for effective action, their purpose solidly grounded in the ideals of the League and the moral sense of the world. Nothing else could arrest approaching war.[17] This proposal, augmented by the view that a continuation of appeasement would mean a series of retreats and surrenders until all of Britain's friends had been 'thrown to the wolves' and she was left to face her fate alone, constituted the central thrust in Churchill's outlook from that point onward, and he pressed it with vigour on many occasions. But his long reputation as a party maverick, and a pugnacious one at that, prevented his views from carrying full weight until the international situation had drastically deteriorated.

As early as the debate on Eden's resignation, dissident Conservatives in the House of Commons began to express displeasure with the government's policy by abstaining in divisions relating to foreign policy approval. Only one, Vyvyan Adams, voted against the government then; but nearly fifty others abstained, and many of those supported an amendment which deplored the circumstances in which Eden had been obliged to resign.[18] The tactic of abstention was repeated at the close of debate on Munich on October 6th. Despite the surge of emotion which swept the nation, most of the prominent Conservatives who were not members of the government abstained from voting on Simon's motion that the House approve the policy by which war had been averted and peace was being sought. Churchill had initially urged a vote

---

[15] For optimistic estimates of Eden's capacity to carry a large number of Conservatives with him had he chosen to challenge Chamberlain openly, see Lewis Broad, *Anthony Eden: the Chronicle of a Career* (New York, 1955), pp. 107–8; and John Connell, *The 'Office': a Study in British Foreign Policy and Its Makers, 1919–1951* (London, 1958), p. 270. But both agree that Eden was not the man even to contemplate such a challenge.

[16] See Richard H. Powers, 'Churchill's Parliamentary Commentary on British Foreign Policy, 1935–1938', *Journal of Modern History* XXVI, no. 2 (1954), pp. 179–82.

[17] *House of Commons Debates*, March 14th, 1938, col. 100.

[18] This group included Edward Spears, Anthony Crossley, J. W. Hills, Sir Derrick Gunston, Paul Emrys-Evans, Harold Macmillan, and J. R. Cartland. *The Times*, February 23rd, 1938.

against the motion, but that was abandoned in view of the lack of faith in the Opposition's position and the hope that Chamberlain would now, after his rude experiences at Hitler's hands, see clearly the necessity for collective action instead of dangerous bargaining with aggressors. Further, it was politically dangerous should Chamberlain call an election. As Amery later explained it, abstention was 'enough to mark our disapproval of the government's policy' without separating the dissident Conservatives 'from the main body whom events would presently bring around to our point of view'.[19]

In the months preceding Munich, dissident Conservatives had warned from time to time that the maintenance of peace required that Britain take a very different direction from Chamberlain's; that decency and respect for international obligations must be squarely upheld; and that repeated demonstrations of magnanimity to bullies defied the rules of logic. Churchill, Anthony Crossley, J. W. Hills, Paul Emrys-Evans, the duchess of Atholl, J. R. Cartland, Duncan Sandys, and Vyvyan Adams advanced such views on one or more occasions, with reference to Anglo-Italian negotiations, British policy towards Spain, and the growing German threat in central Europe. Churchill in particular emphasized the need to stand firmly by France in defence of Czechoslovakia. The events of September induced a flurry of activity among the dissident Conservatives, who tried to stiffen government policy through Churchill's and Eden's personal contacts, since parliament was not in session. Especially notable was their deep concern for securing Russian support, which emphasized the triumph of vital national interests over traditional party prejudice. But they lacked a common, clear-cut policy and the assurance of wide support in the Commons; and their activity had little effect on Chamberlain's course of action.

Munich jelled, enlarged, and strengthened dissident Conservative criticism of appeasement. It prompted the resignation of a second cabinet minister, Duff Cooper, first lord of the admiralty, who no longer thought it possible to reach a reasonable settlement with Hitler and foresaw the need for Britain to stand and fight in order to prevent his domination of Europe by force. Eden and Cranborne renewed their warnings against 'stand and deliver' diplomacy, Churchill thundered against the policy of uninterrupted retreat, Law acidly protested Britain's apparent intention to support, as a junior partner, Germany's domination of the continent, and Amery, long an opponent of colonial but not continental appeasement, enjoined the government to abandon its 'go-as-you-please' attitude and seek the mutual cooperation of 'any other freedom-loving nation which cares to work with us'. They all appealed for a 'great national effort', a concept which, though ill-defined, connoted a conscious endeavour to alert the British people to the dangers ahead and the sacrifices they would surely be asked to

[19] L. S. Amery, *My Political Life* (London, 1955), III, p. 287.

make in order to meet them.[20] Beyond the vocal dissenters there was a broadening range of government supporters who experienced deepening disquiet, as well as humiliation, over the Munich settlement and the implications of Chamberlain's diplomacy there. Few backbench regulars were prepared to endorse the settlement in the Commons. The predominant sentiment was one of acute relief that war had been averted, but not enthusiasm about the manner or confidence in the future. And the final defiant gesture of twenty-two dissident Conservatives, nearly all of those on the government benches known for their particular interest in foreign affairs, in remaining seated in the Chamber while the House divided on Simon's motion of October 6th, was sufficient to rattle even the cabinet.

But resistance to the government was risky and the dissident Conservatives knew it. Munich seemed popular in the country. There was extensive talk of a new election and the replacement of dissenters with reliable Tory candidates. There was more than the usual pressure on constituency chairmen from the Conservative central office to control, or abandon, dissenters. There was talk of a split in the party, with all the uncertainties which that would entail. So in the months following Munich dissident Conservatives had to tread carefully 'if they wanted to stay in the party, keep their seats in the House of Commons, and thereby retain the chance of influencing future policy, getting into office, and capturing the party machinery'.[21] The surface calm which prevailed in Europe for a time thereafter enabled them to do so, though there were nonetheless intermittent occasions when some of them spoke out publicly against the continuing dangers of appeasement and the need for a decisive change of direction.

The German seizure of Prague, compounded by Chamberlain's wholly inadequate response to it, provoked a veritable revolution in party, and public, opinion. Their position suddenly strengthened by events which had proved them right, dissident Conservatives lashed out at appeasement with new intensity. And now others listened. As all the 'tadpoles' started swimming toward the other pond,[22] Chamberlain confronted a hard decision to undertake policy modification or face party and parliamentary insurrection. He chose to explore the former, and thus began the fitful manoeuvring which culminated in the unilateral guarantee to Poland and the reluctant opening of negotiations with Russia.

The resulting mutations in government policy greatly enhanced the influence of the dissident Conservatives. Men who only days before had been derided within their own party now commanded a new respect.

[20] *House of Commons Debates*, October 3–6th, 1939, col. 31–40, 79–88, 110–14, 199–207, 232–6, 360–73.
[21] Thompson, *The Anti-Appeasers*, p. 195.
[22] To paraphrase Harold Nicolson's diary entry of March 17th, in *Diaries and Letters, 1930–1939* (London, 1967), p. 393.

Using their novel condition to full advantage, they urged the government towards a new peace front against aggression, pressed for the introduction of conscription, faster rearmament, and a broadening of the National government as evidence of Britain's earnestness, adamantly opposed a Polish Munich, and generally counselled firmness in any future dealings with the dictators. Churchill and Eden remained the leading, but certainly not the only spokesmen in the Commons, the latter becoming somewhat bolder than he had been in 1938, the former somewhat more restrained in the expectation of an invitation to join the government, which finally came on September 1st. Duff Cooper wrote a regular column for the *Evening Standard*. Their strained relations with the party were not at once forgotten, but the dissident Conservatives no longer needed to fear party reprisals or public derision. They kept up considerable pressure on the prime minister and their contribution to the resolve with which the nation at length confronted war was most assuredly great.

No cooperation in opposing appeasement was ever effected between the Labour and Liberal parties on one hand and the dissident Conservatives on the other, a fact which surely weakened their impact. While standing on similar ground in foreign policy debates, they went their separate ways in the everyday operation of politics. Eden refused to engage in factious opposition to the government. Churchill, whose call for a 'grand alliance' gave definite form to the vague Labour-Liberal demand for collective security, was not amenable to the general cause of the Left. And Labour's position on rearmament left him dumbfounded. The Labour leaders lacked national stature, and their general socialistic policy had not yet fired the popular imagination. In short, these groups which had come together on issues of diplomacy and were agreed that the Government's policy lacked both principle and expediency, were too divided on other matters to develop an effective cooperative effort. Several limited attempts were made, notably in the wake of Munich, but nothing came of them.[23]

Note must also be made of a handful of earnest critics in the House of Lords. Debate there was less frequent, often less intense, and certainly less significant politically than that in the House of Commons. But it was still another forum in which critics could be heard, not without some hope of influence since the foreign secretary, after March 1938, was a member of the Lords. Chief among the critics throughout 1938–39 was Lord Snell, a former Labour MP and a member of the council of the Royal Institute of International Affairs. He was often supported most vociferously by Lord Strabolgi, opposition chief whip, and

---

[23] Amery–Attlee and Macmillan–Dalton conversations explored the possibilities. Amery attributes failure to Labour's refusal to tolerate Chamberlain as prime minister. *My Political Life* III, pp. 298–9. Dalton cites the division and uncertainty within dissident Conservative ranks. *The Fateful Years*, pp. 199–207. Sir Stafford Cripps' abortive personal efforts to create a 'popular front' early in 1939 had neither Labour party nor dissident Conservative support.

Viscount Cecil of Chelwood, one-time Conservative MP and champion of the League of Nations. Their pointed commentary, occasionally punctuated by sharp expressions of doubt about appeasement from a few others, including the archbishop of Canterbury on several crucial occasions, gave testimony to the fact that there was a dissenting point of view in the Lords, and prompted Halifax to exercise considerable care in explaining policy developments there. It was in this context that the difference in emphasis between Chamberlain and Halifax concerning the nature of appeasement (see p. 58) was most apparent.

A potentially significant pocket of opposition to appeasement was located in the foreign office itself. First, there were those officials, including Robert Vansittart (permanent under-secretary until early 1938; thereafter chief diplomatic advisor), Sir Orme Sargent (assistant under-secretary), and Reginald Leeper (counsellor), who advocated a policy of containment toward Germany. Doubting that even a whole-sale meeting of Germany's grievances would blunt her expansionist penchant, and fearing that such a course would only induce France to make separate arrangements with Germany, they looked to expanded rearmament, strengthened ties with the French, and friendly relations with the Russians as the best deterrent. Some officials closely associated with Eden favoured a policy of keeping Germany, as well as Italy, off-balance and guessing, and assuming a posture of firmness short of rigid commitment while ultimately relying on rearmament to give force to their position. Among those remaining after Eden's resignation was Oliver Harvey, who continued as private secretary to the foreign minister.[24] Hardly anyone in the foreign office accepted Chamberlain's opinion that it was possible to come to a general and lasting arrangement with the dictators without an exceptional rearmament effort on Britain's part.[25]

But foreign office opposition never reached its full potential. With the office seriously divided within itself, Chamberlain's conviction that he must work around it rather than through it was periodically reinforced. Vansittart, whose outspoken anti-Germanism was unacceptable to Chamberlain, was 'promoted' to a high-sounding position in which he was isolated from the policy-making process. The influence of the Eden group, suffering from the disadvantage that its policy was long-term and cautious, declined proportionately after his departure from office. Warnings about Germany from both the foreign office and British representatives abroad, particularly Sir Howard Kennard, ambassador in Warsaw and a disbeliever in appeasement, were apparently blunted by the extensive administrative control of Sir Warren Fisher, permanent secretary of the treasury and head of the civil service, who was able to influence the submission of foreign office

[24] See John Harvey (editor), *The Diplomatic Diaries of Oliver Harvey, 1937–1940* (London, 1970).
[25] *The Memoirs of Lord Gladwyn*, p. 75.

advice to the cabinet. Yet the anti-appeasement element by no means disappeared. There remained in Whitehall middle-rank officials, like Sargent and Leeper, whose persistent warnings undoubtedly tempered foreign office positions and exerted as yet unmeasured, and perhaps unmeasurable, influence on Halifax and others at critical moments.[26]

Within the cabinet there were certain ministers with latent reservations about appeasement which surfaced occasionally when Hitler's or Mussolini's actions became especially difficult to tolerate (see p. 60). On the issue of negotiations with Italy, which led to Eden's resignation, Chamberlain himself noted that four of his colleagues supported him 'with some qualification or reserve'.[27] But it was not until the Czech crisis neared a climax that rumblings were heard in significant proportions. Some sympathy for firmness toward Germany as the best means to deter war was expressed by a few cabinet members, Duff Cooper in particular, at a meeting on August 30th. Then between Chamberlain's visits to Berchtesgaden and Munich at least a half dozen ministers, notably the younger ones, balked at accepting Hitler's demands. At one point (September 25th) five or six of them toyed with the idea of resigning if the Godesberg terms were accepted. And several others, Halifax in the forefront, Hailsham behind him, stood for rejection of those conditions. The upshot was delay in recommending acceptance to the Czechs, as Chamberlain proposed, and his initiation of one final effort to reach a compromise with Hitler. When Munich was concluded, all except Duff Cooper quietly acquiesced in the prime minister's solution, persuaded in the end that there was no better alternative. But Oliver Stanley, Earl Winterton, Earl De La Warr, Malcolm MacDonald, Leslie Hore-Belisha, and Walter Elliot, as well as Halifax himself, had given expression to innate misgivings about the limits to which appeasement could rightfully go.[28]

After Munich, cabinet composition involved a narrowing range of minds. Duff Cooper departed, De La Warr was demoted from lord privy seal to the board of education, and in January Winterton was dismissed. Their successors, Lord Stanhope, Sir John Anderson, and W. S. Morrison respectively, were somewhat more like-minded with Chamberlain. Only Stanley, MacDonald, Elliot, and Hore-Belisha, in a cabinet of 23 ministers, remained to provide some leaven to debate. Even so, there were other occasions when cabinet pressure, not exactly opposition, on Chamberlain materially affected his outlook. While

[26] It is now well established that Cadogan, himself suddenly converted to firmness, persuaded Halifax to reject Hitler's Godesberg demands on September 25th, 1938. See *The Diaries of Sir Alexander Cadogan*, pp. 103–5.
[27] Macleod, *Neville Chamberlain*, p. 216.
[28] See Middlemas, *Diplomacy of Illusion*, pp. 314–16, 347ff.; Colvin, *The Chamberlain Cabinet*, pp. 154–67; Rock, *Appeasement on Trial*, pp. 120–22, 127. Middlemas describes cabinet discussions during these weeks in great detail. In *Beaverbrook* (London and New York, 1972), pp. 385–6, A. J. P. Taylor presents evidence suggesting that Duff Cooper, too, would not have gone through with his threatened resignation had Chamberlain permitted it.

the cabinet's first reaction to the German coup in Czechoslovakia was to play down its significance, a number of ministers understood the signs of parliamentary and party revolt and encouraged Chamberlain's rapid change in position. The adoption of conscription in late April, quite against the prime minister's will, owed much to Hore-Belisha's persistence, at the risk of his political life. The continuation of negotiations with Russia, when Chamberlain was sorely tempted to abandon them, drew considerable support from some of his cabinet colleagues, especially Halifax and Hoare.[29] That the signing of the Nazi-Soviet pact should have no effect whatever on Britain's commitment to Poland reflected settled cabinet sentiment. And the anxious, late-night urgings of at least half the members of the cabinet, perplexed by Chamberlain's failure on September 2nd to invoke the Polish guarantee by declaring war on Germany, were crucial in closing any avenue to last-minute defection from the nation's pledged word. In all of these instances, however, cabinet pressures paralleled those arising from parliament and the party so that their relative decisiveness is very difficult to weigh.

Until mid-1938, the British press reacted to appeasement largely along partisan political lines. Criticism emanated mainly from journals with Labour and Liberal leanings and a few independent journals, such as the *Financial News* and the *Glasgow Herald*. As the Czech crisis developed, some Conservative papers, notably the *Daily Telegraph*, also began to evince misgivings about excessive concessions, and independent journals tended more toward support for 'a policy of firmness'. But their views were usually set in general terms. After Munich all sections of the press expressed profound relief that war had been averted, but a sense of humiliation and dishonour, a growing suspicion about appeasement, and apprehension about the future were also generally evident amid a broader tone of suspended judgement. Then Hitler's occupation of Prague ignited an explosive demand for a firmer policy toward the dictators, whatever its specific form and nature. Illustrative of this was the suddenly altered tone of the influential independent *Observer*, whose editor, J. L. Garvin, a Chamberlain intimate, had previously viewed appeasement with an airy optimism. Now the paper insisted on a radical change in the temper of the British government. Even the Conservative *Daily Mail*, which had long endorsed appeasement from an isolationist, non-entanglement viewpoint, waxed impatient for action on new and different lines. This demand continued in the press generally at only a slightly fluctuating level of intensity, though in various forms, including support for an alliance with Russia and clamour for Churchill's inclusion in the cabinet, until the outbreak of war; it suggests that the press, as well as the public generally, was considerably ahead of the government in its recognition of the failure of appeasement. And while the press as a whole never became a united agent of anti-

[29] Despite Hoare's association with appeasement, Colvin holds that 'most of what Hoare said in cabinet has stood up to the test of time'. *The Chamberlain Cabinet*, p. 185.

appeasement, it was instrumental, after March 1939, in pressing the need for new initiatives and creating a climate in which they would be widely accepted.[30]

Finally, there were in Britain some organizations, pressure groups, or other 'agencies' which stood if not in direct opposition to appeasement at least in a questioning posture toward it. The League of Nations Union, for example, generally decried the rejection of the League as the most appropriate agency through which to resolve the problems besetting Europe. But its members were divided on the issue of treaty revision and the prospects of appeasing Germany. The Next Five Years Group, whose members included Sir Arthur Salter, one of the most consistent opponents of appeasement, Norman Angell, and Lord Allen of Hurtwood, stood staunchly for collective security, with Germany, if she was prepared to cooperate, but if not, without her. It specifically rejected the isolationist posture of another group, later labelled New Imperialists, who shunned continental ties and recognized no British interests in central or eastern Europe. The New Commonwealth supported armed collective security through an international force controlled by the League; while Focus for the Defence of Freedom and Peace, composed of prominent persons of all political affiliations, campaigned for the famous 'arms and the Covenant' theme. In another vein, protest arose from professional historians and journalists who published books and articles which challenged the validity of appeasement.[31] Even the savage jibes of David Low, popular cartoonist of the *Evening Standard*, carried poignant overtones of appeasement criticism.[32] But such sources of protest carried hardly any influence. Chamberlain's cabinet was highly sensitive to the political realities of the party system but not to pressure groups beyond the House of Commons.[33]

In summary, not all critics of appeasement looked at the policy in the same way. Most of the dissident Conservatives, for example, felt considerable sympathy for France, a disposition to share her long-standing suspicion of Germany, and a conviction that revision of Versailles should not be considered, if at all, under Nazi threats of violence. A much stronger effort at national rearmament was clearly required. On the other hand, Labour critics showed considerable sympathy for Russia and open diplomacy in which she might participate, as well as solicitude for the Republican cause in Spain. But national rearmament was resisted on both ideological and partisan grounds. Then, too, there were a limited number of critics who opposed appeasement on a basis of

---

[30] For more detail on the press, and reference to specific newspapers, see Rock, *Appeasement on Trial*, and Gannon, *The British Press and Germany, 1936–1939*.

[31] Examples are R. W. Seton-Watson, *Britain and the Dictators* (London, 1938); Elizabeth Wiskemann, *Czechs and Germans* (London, 1938); and G. E. R. Gedye, *Fallen Bastions* (London, 1939). Seton-Watson and S. Grant Duff stand out among those who wrote such items for periodicals.

[32] Of course, there were many prominent persons in various walks of life aside from politics who came to doubt appeasement or adjudge it wholly mistaken.

[33] Middlemas, *Diplomacy of Illusion*, p. 7, *passim*.

continental non-involvement and isolationism. Among most of the critics, however, there was general attachment to the concept of collective security and the League of Nations. Only through a strengthening of these could the treacherous dictators be confronted effectively and their aggressive tendencies blunted.

Since appeasement, in essence, involved the reestablishment of a concert of Europe directed by the four great powers, Britain, France, Germany, and Italy, it implied extensive reorientation in France's security system, the exclusion of Russia from participation in the affairs of Europe, and the abandonment of collective security through the League. These approaches to practical politics were all rejected by most of the critics, isolationists again excluded, who believed in the need to work for a balance of power, to make and maintain continental commitments, and to utilize the methods of traditional diplomacy. There were also moral dimensions involved. Appeasement seemed to reject whatever progress had been made since 1919 in the development of a peaceful system of international relations. The promotion of Germany and Italy to full participation in the hegemony of Europe appeared to imply that ruthlessness and immorality were being rewarded. The condoning of violations by force of international law seemed a curious way to ensure the long-term cooperation and good behaviour of the fascist powers. Further, the critics' dislike of appeasement as a policy was enhanced by other elements both incidental and essential to it—Chamberlain's stony personality, his rigid self-confidence, and the irregular methods which he employed. Thus appeasement was seen first as a risky adventure, then as dangerous collusion, at length as treacherous betrayal.

7 Appeasement in Historical Perspective

British appeasement in the 1930s will no doubt constitute a topic for debate, at least among scholars, as long as men are interested in their history. Related as it is to the coming of the Second World War, which sealed the demotion of Europe after a millenium as the prime mover in world affairs, it is not likely to decline quickly in interest and importance. Like most great issues in the human experience, it will be variously interpreted, even after the generation which directly experienced it is gone. No real consensus may emerge, no 'final judgement' seems possible. Yet tentative reflection and evaluation are essential, and they may appropriately be attempted here.

The ultimate judgement on appeasement does not rest on the essential nature of the policy alone. It depends in part on the broader context in which it was pursued, particularly on the view taken of German policy after November 1937. If Hitler was bent on a programme of aggression designed to achieve German hegemony over Europe, then active appeasement was futile from the start. But if Hitler was basically an opportunist, pursuing the traditional objectives of German foreign policy, knowing when to proceed and when to halt according to the positions assumed by potential adversaries, then it becomes a matter of identifying points in time where ignorance or ineptitude led to wrong decisions or when different policies might have halted the Führer's advance.[1] It does seem clear that Hitler at first felt a curious respect for Britain and envisaged a place for her in his own scheme of things. But when the British failed to live up to his expectations and requirements, he abandoned his earlier regard, assigned them to the enemy camp, and lost interest in striking any

---

[1] The historical debate over Hitler's policy, in which A. J. P. Taylor has been the leading spokesman of the 'revisionist' view, is conveniently summarized in William Roger Louis, (editor), *The Origins of the Second World War: A. J. P. Taylor and His Critics* (New York, 1972). Alan Bullock, an authority on Hitler, believes that the Führer was both a crazy fanatic and a cynical opportunist. He was each in turn, his foreign policy combining consistency of aim with complete opportunism in method and tactics. Bullock also doubts that war with Germany could have been avoided, unless Britain and France were prepared to concede German hegemony over all of Europe east of the Rhine. His views, presented in a Raleigh Lecture, appear on pp. 117–45 of the Louis volume and are cited in Arthur Marwick, *The Nature of History* (London, 1970; New York, 1971), p. 317.

deals with them. This point apparently had been reached by early 1938 In this sense, Chamberlain's efforts were distinctly too little, too late, and active appeasement was a policy improvised after the initiative had passed to Germany.[2]

Hitler was not, of course, easy to fathom, nor were his actions simple to forecast. Despite the rantings of *Mein Kampf*, the violations of Versailles, and the ominous German interference in Spanish and Austrian politics, the future direction of his policy and the chances of ameliorating German relations with the rest of Europe, and Britain in particular, were by no means certain in London or elsewhere by the end of 1937. Further, the prevailing temper in Britain clearly favoured honest efforts to pacify Germany and thus remove a most troublesome thorn which had festered in the European body politic ever since Versailles. The attitude reflected a curious and possibly unique trait of the British national character—indulgence in a guilt complex with regard to her history. When others make trouble for them, the British sometimes, instinctively perhaps, are persuaded that they are really to blame. Thus there were misgivings about the First World War and Versailles as Hitler began to assert himself. It was as if British perfidy was taken to be the root cause of Nazi petulance, which could now be assuaged only by acts of benevolence and good-will inspired by remorse. This sentiment was clearly evident in Britain's acceptance, almost with satisfaction, to the complete bewilderment of France, of Hitler's occupation of the Rhineland. It also tempered, to a large degree, the British attitude towards German actions in Austria and Czechoslovakia.[3] In conjunction with a broader and deeper 'crisis of the liberal conscience', the liberal legacy of the World War which took the form of universal determination that it must never happen again,[4] it constituted an influential ingredient in British thought.

This is not to say that public sentiment led inexorably to the policy of appeasement, or that appeasement was the only policy possible in the circumstances of the time. The British government simply and honestly believed that appeasement was the most effective policy it could devise on the basis of the evidence at hand. And this, rather than some theory of devious calculation, doctrinaire commitment, or shameful cowardice, constitutes the best, if seemingly simplistic, explanation for the general course of policy which it followed. But the existence of an extensive popular sympathy for appeasement made it much easier than it would otherwise have been for those in authority to work their will, and provides the basis for contending that 'if . . . the "appeasers" were

---

[2] See Middlemas, *Diplomacy of Illusion*, pp. 157–80, for a summary of recent scholarship on the development of German policy.

[3] See Amery, *My Political Life* III, p. 247.

[4] F. R. Gannon cites as perhaps the major conclusion of his book on *The British Press and Germany, 1936–1939*, that 'appeasement was . . . the product of a crisis of the liberal conscience.' p. 4.

wrong, so was the great bulk of British public opinion which supported them, with more or less enthusiasm, until the last days of peace.'[5]

It can be argued that appeasement was a symptom of Britain's declining world position and an essential response to it. The balance of world power was potentially unfavourable to her from the First World War onwards, and the diminished resources of the nation seemed to require a technique of striving for compromise abroad. A basically conservative outlook towards the prevailing international order, assumptions about the primacy of economic issues, and preoccupation with social problems trebly reinforced this apparent necessity. So Chamberlain's government might be commended for accepting Britain's diminished place of power and influence in the world and for its efforts to bring the nation's strength and commitments more closely into line, an arduous endeavour which eventually consumed the energies of British statesmen for several decades after 1945. But it is remarkable how little these limitations on British policy were recognized, or even understood, by those in positions of political responsibility in the 1930s. Consequently, there are clear limits to how far these factors may be cited as conscious considerations in appeasement, and this no doubt helps to explain the extent to which they have been ignored by the critics of appeasement ever since.

Appeasement was certainly not an 'evil' policy in its initial conception. It was not a coward's creed or a silly, treacherous notion advanced alone by stupid men. Rather, its principal tenet of concessions through strength was a noble concept rooted in the moral and religious traditions of the English people, reinforced by a certain cultural sophistication, courage, and common sense. But it was increasingly unrealistic as applied to Nazi Germany during 1938–39, so that it suffered progressive distortion and eventual failure. This was largely a matter of deficient judgement, not sinister intentions, on the part of responsible leaders, a failure to adjust ideas born of one period to the changing circumstances and requirements of another. In one sense, the policy involved a defiance of probabilities since the dictators had hardly demonstrated generosity and reasonableness in their actions and attitudes of previous years. Yet any practical estimate of the diplomatic situation as late as 1937 seemed to point to the fact that appeasement, at least of a limited and exploratory kind, was worth attempting. Men and movements have been known to change when the circumstances in which they function are altered. And if many Germans incorrectly calculated the nature of Hitler and the Nazi movement (which appears to be an incontrovertible fact), it is easy to see how Englishmen, further removed from the scene and conditioned by a wholly different set of values, would also fail at once to grasp the evil and dangerous essence of the man and the movement.

The point at which the appeasers become most vulnerable to

[5] Northedge, *The Troubled Giant*, p. 617.

criticism is in their refusal to alter or abandon the policy in favour of some new departure as overpowering evidence began to accumulate that appeasement simply was not accomplishing its purpose. Just when the breaking point may be said to have arrived is open to interpretation. It may not be stretching credulity too far, however, to submit that the general policy toward the crisis in Czechoslovakia, even acceptance of the much despised Munich agreement, are both understandable and defensible in the light of Britain's poor military posture, the stern warnings against war which came from the British chiefs of staff, the lack of support from the dominions, the fitful irresolution of France, the potency of the argument for Sudeten self-determination, and so on. But after Munich it is a different matter. To go on blithely preaching appeasement and exuding confidence in the imminent arrival of a 'new era', to go on asserting faith and trust in the dictators, publicly at least, despite the harrowing experiences of September at Hitler's hands and the glut of intelligence about possible German aggression which poured into London during the months which followed,[6] is difficult to fathom and impossible to defend. In this, the appeasers did a great disservice to the English people, deluding them about the newly apparent nature of Hitler and the Nazi menace, undermining their own credibility about the urgency of rearmament, and blunting any revival of will to resist further totalitarian encroachment to which the practical political sensibilities of many Englishmen now pointed.

That the 'peace psychosis' of the English people still circumscribed the government's freedom of action is a debatable proposition. It is true that the great majority of Englishmen, emotionally overcome by release from war, welcomed Chamberlain home from Munich as the saviour of peace and civilization, but the hysteria of Munich lasted only a few days. The sense of relief was quickly modified by feelings of guilt and humiliation, and the frightening recollection of digging slit trenches in public parks and trying on gas masks in anticipation of a German air attack created a powerful undercurrent of anxiety on which a new policy orientation might well have capitalized. It was an opportune time for a new initiative to meet the threat which by now should have been obvious to all who prided themselves on realism, as the proponents of appeasement consistently did. But Chamberlain and his colleagues left the nation devoid of constructive leadership at a time when it was desperately needed, lulling it back to the slumber of false security when it should have been rapidly awakening to stark reality.

Some would say that the 'breaking point' in appeasement should have come well in advance of Munich. There is no denying the

---

[6] Much of the intelligence was suppressed or underestimated. Sidney Aster, *1939: the Making of the Second World War* (New York, 1973), pp. 51–6; *The Memoirs of Lord Gladwyn*, pp. 80, 83–7. Lord Gladwyn adds: 'Never . . . could any government have been more fully warned of the prospective conduct of an adversary.'

appeasers' basic errors of judgement which preceded that occasion. One of these was the assumption that Hitler, and Mussolini, would act on the same rational plane on which appeasement moved. They failed to grasp the essence of fascist totalitarianism, its necessity to expand, and its ability, indeed readiness, to mobilize the nation for aggression and even war against Britain and France. They failed to understand that Nazism assaulted the very combination of reason and morality out of which appeasement was conceived. In this sense, the appeasers were 'deficient in their analysis of human nature'[7] and the logic of appeasement was mistaken. But discarding rational assumptions as out of place in a violent world was never a part of appeasement's style and temper.

More specifically, Chamberlain's credulity and his devious methods in arranging conversations with Italy seem remarkable in extent and distasteful in manner. Eden certainly thought so and resigned. But if Mussolini had moved militarily to counter the *Anschluss*, a seeming possibility in view of the importance which Italy had long attached to Austrian independence, Chamberlain's behaviour would most likely have been vindicated. Thus the failure of the government to reevaluate the European situation after the *Anschluss* was clearly more important. Here a major chance for stock-taking, particularly appropriate because of the obvious flagrance of the German action and the startling effect which it had on many Englishmen and Europeans generally, was brushed aside and forgotten. Whether or not one accepts Ian Colvin's contention that 'the inference is strong that Austria should have been the storm signal and Czechoslovakia the casus belli',[8] the appeasers' complacent response to that act of German aggression leaves one wondering about the extent to which appeasement, a state of mind as well as a policy, had already become a passion prompting its devotees to ignore any evidence which did not suit their purpose.

At the very least this unsettling development might have stimulated a thorough review and upward revision of Britain's rearmament efforts. There was, in fact, a good deal of talk about the need for this, but little action resulted. Thus another error of judgement committed by the appeasers was their deliberate neglect of defence requirements, mainly in response to treasury admonitions. This placed an undue burden for national defence on foreign policy and practically assured the distortion of appeasement as a policy of reasonable, limited concessions made from a position of strength. It is true that the nation laboured with scarce resources and a public opinion distrustful of armaments. But adequate programmes were not even considered, nor the large parliamentary majority put to the test. Even Munich failed to generate radical change in this regard. So the military thinking of the Chamberlain government directly refuted the theory, later

[7] Lanyi, 'The Problem of Appeasement', p. 321.
[8] *The Chamberlain Cabinet*, p. 269.

propounded, that appeasement was a policy devised to gain time for rearmament. And the cabinet records lay that proposition finally to rest.

There is conflicting evidence about the appeasers' perception of the Czechoslovak crisis. Chamberlain and others seemed to believe that Sudeten self-determination was a fundamental issue, and that it would be folly to risk a war in defiance of so highly regarded and widely accepted a principle. Yet Lord Butler testifies in his memoirs that Chamberlain was fully aware that the Sudeten problem might not be the real issue and that Hitler might have far larger ambitions.[9] In any case, this much seems clear: there was no deliberate plan to turn Germany eastward, though the possible benefits of this had no doubt crossed many a mind and even been hinted openly; and the government's attitude toward Czechoslovakia might best be characterized as indifferent. As Middlemas observes, it was the horror of war which made Hitler's quarrel with Czechs a British interest, not concern for Czechoslovakia itself.[10] And as the crisis unfolded, the importance of clearing the way for a larger Anglo-German settlement overshadowed everything else. The appeasers clung to the illusions that central Europe could be pacified if Prague made enough concessions, and that successful resolution of the Sudeten problem would mark a crucial turning point in Anglo-German relations. Thus Chamberlain's failure to bargain for Hitler's assurance of this—a condition for which alone the Czech sacrifice would be worth making—was later identified by Hoare and others as the greatest mistake of all. Even a warning to Hitler about the possible consequences of his aggressive intentions, which Hitler apparently expected, might have been useful. But the oft-repeated and persuasive argument that Czechoslovakia could not be reconstituted, even after a victorious war, prevailed, even though it neglected the broader strategic impact of the expansion of German power in central Europe and missed the point that the freeing of Europe from German threats, not the maintenance or reestablishment of Czechoslovakia, was the basic issue at stake.[11]

In a very real sense, the Runciman mission constituted Britain's 'last exercise in positive appeasement'. Thereafter, appeasement became 'a nervous, jerky, guilt-encumbered affair; not a confident philosophy, but a painful surrender to threats'.[12] Chamberlain's manipulation of Runciman's report[13] reinforces the point that the pacification of Hitler

---

[9] *The Art of the Possible*, p. 65. Butler was under-secretary of state for foreign affairs, 1938–41.

[10] *Diplomacy of Illusion*, p. 369.

[11] See Bruegel, *Czechoslovakia Before Munich*, p. 195. Messages from 'opposition' elements in Germany suggesting Hitler's broader objectives and the need for a strong warning were not weighed extensively, nor did they figure importantly in policy-making. The British found it difficult to assess the strength and reliability of the anti-Nazi resistance.

[12] Gilbert, *The Roots of Appeasement*, pp. 174–5.

[13] See Bruegel, *Czechoslovakia Before Munich*, pp. 274–8.

was the central objective to which everything else was subordinated. Thus Munich was not a climax, except in a very emotional sense, but merely another stage of development in the forces and assumptions governing British policy.

The controversy over Munich will never be settled. It is too easy to take alternative views and accumulate arguments to support them. Thus it comes down to a matter of feeling and instinct rather than reason and logic. That Munich was essentially inescapable, even wise, given the circumstances of September 1938, is a weighty proposition. But that Britain should never have fallen into that predicament is also quite compelling. Whether Britain would have done better to have fought, if necessary, in 1938 instead of waiting until one year later may be debated endlessly, both with regard to her military preparation relative to Germany's and the extent to which Munich was essential to educating the British in the ways of depraved men and therefore basic to their later conviction that war, as never before in history, was right. But to put excessive emphasis on the 'validity' of Munich is to miss a broader point about it as an extension of appeasement. Whether Munich was right or wrong, it was a shameful, humiliating, alarming experience.[14] And for Chamberlain and some of his colleagues to interpret it as a constructive accomplishment on the way to peace with justice and reconciliation with Germany was downright deceitful, especially since the prime minister himself was not convinced that Munich had made peace any more secure. After Munich, appeasement was a clearly misguided, and misguiding, policy.

There was almost nothing, after Munich, to suggest that appeasement had any chance of success with Germany. On the other hand, there was much to suggest the conclusive failure of Anglo-German reconciliation. Halifax presented such information, in the form of a series of intelligence reports, to the foreign policy committee, in its first meeting since June, in mid-November; and the weeks which followed produced abundant evidence of German and Italian contempt for Britain and her role in Europe. But the British policy outlook did not change. There was not even a serious canvassing of alternative courses of action. It was as if the government was incapable of seeing alternatives to appeasement. Still moved by the vision of a permanent settlement, it was more intent upon justifying continuation of the old policy than weighing alternative courses. As Middlemas aptly puts it, 'admission that Munich was a bare escape from the pit, followed by the preparations eventually made in March 1939, might have saved more than that government's reputation.'[15] But Hitler's intentions were thoroughly miscalculated, on

[14] That the crisis was caused by Hitler's deliberate inflation of the Sudeten problem was painfully apparent at the time. The dissecting of an independent nation without its participation in the deliberations was a distressing departure from the normal course of international relations. The absence of adequate preparations for the conference was awkward and disconcerting.

[15] *Diplomacy of Illusion*, p. 457.

grounds which still defy logical explanation, inasmuch as all the evidence pointed to the opposite conclusion. And appeasement remained unmodified until later events quite literally forced its change, against the government's will.

The German conquest of Prague was a shocking development for all Englishmen, whatever their previous policy preferences. Chamberlain, initially more concerned to defend and 'protect' appeasement than to see new dangers in what had happened, was forced into new interpretations, and consequently new policy initiatives, by a groundswell of impatience and anxiety which swept through parliament, the press, and the public at large. Most of those around him, the foreign office, the service chiefs, and members of his own cabinet and party, took the destruction of Czechoslovakia much more seriously than did the prime minister. The eventual result, after a cautious British scheme to associate France, Russia, and Poland in a joint declaration of consultation had aborted, was the guarantee to Poland.

That guarantee was a most decisive measure, crucial to the course of appeasement. Only 'an improvisation'[16] drafted by Chamberlain, Halifax, and Cadogan on the afternoon of March 30th, a 'more or less instinctive reaction'[17] to the pressing need to do something to deter Hitler, the guarantee was evidently not intended to forswear appeasement generally or to make extensive, permanent change in the policy of noncommitment. While the ultimate objectives to be gained by the action were not carefully calculated, it was intended no doubt to meet an imperative public demand that Poland should not be permitted to go the same way as Czechoslovakia, and beyond that, to put a significant obstacle in Hitler's way, to warn him firmly of the limits of Britain's tolerance and credulity, and hopefully to incline him more readily toward negotiating that broader settlement which would henceforth render such seemingly radical policy departures unnecessary. It was not the substance of Germany's demands on Poland or the merits of the German case which prompted the guarantee. It was the cumulative evidence of Germany's apparent intention to dominate Europe by force, which had reached a point where it now required some act of defiance. Appreciation of this need to act, irrespective of practical considerations, best explains why the guarantee was extended, even though it had little military justification and radically reduced the range of diplomatic movement. A political creation devoid of effective preparation for a general war,[18] the guarantee was essentially a bluff except in the sense that Britain was now committed to halting Hitlerian aggression whatever the consequences.

---

[16] Lord Strang, *Home and Abroad* (London, 1956), p. 161.

[17] *The Memoirs of Lord Gladwyn*, p. 92.

[18] The first appreciable upswing in British armaments production coincided with the guarantee to Poland. This may have reassured Chamberlain—see W. N. Medlicott, *British Foreign Policy since Versailles, 1919–1963* (London, 1968). p. 202—but had limited strategic impact.

The guarantee to Poland committed Britain to Poland's defence and her territorial integrity, through the pledging of her word and thus her honour, to a far greater extent than the government initially planned or realized. It marked, in fact, the end of appeasement insofar as its applicability to German demands on Warsaw were concerned. When Hitler chose to move against Poland late in August, the British government's hands were tied. The nation at large simply would not tolerate any tampering with its solemnly pledged word; concessions inspired by appeasement were clearly out of the question. Thus, ironically, appeasement met its end in an unintended manner, in sharp contrast to the careful planning which had gone into the early stages of the policy's formulation.

By the guarantees to Poland, Greece, and Rumania, Britain practically assured that association with Russia, now sorely tempted to sit back and do nothing, would be very difficult except on her own terms. But the government was prepared to face that prospect. Warnings about the effect of such guarantees on Russia's position, and reminders from the chiefs of staff that Russia alone could assist the Poles militarily, were suppressed or disregarded by the cabinet.[19] The attitude toward Russia was that she really did not matter much. Poland was still considered the key, so there would be no point in seeking Soviet assistance if Poland and Rumania were alienated by it, as they clearly said they would be. The government's great concern for the 'feelings' of Poland, in view of its earlier disregard for the 'feelings' of Czechoslovakia, not to mention Russia, can be explained only in terms of faulty presuppositions. Beyond that, the government simply was not thinking in military terms. An arrangement with Russia, like the guarantee to Poland, would be mainly a diplomatic ploy. The aim of a peace front was not to prepare for military action but to induce Germany to the conference table. Hitler must be deterred, not challenged. To this end, Soviet assistance was considered a convenience but nothing more.

In their failure to see in Nazism a greater danger than they feared from Russia, while concomitantly disregarding Russia as a potentially significant factor in European affairs, the proponents of appeasement committed errors of judgement which inevitably retarded the course of negotiations with Russia from mid-April to mid-August 1939. The Russians were considerably less than engaging in the way they conducted the negotiations, disparaging British efforts to meet their wishes, refusing to compromise, and occasionally raising new points and difficulties. But the British were wrong to treat the Russians like suppliants, to open the conversations with proposals which were ludicrous and humiliating, to haggle unduly about every concession, thus weakening their already weak credibility, and to refuse to send a major minister to Moscow to bolster the sagging talks. They could not seem to understand that Soviet mistrust of British policy was, for some

[19] See Aster, *1939*, pp. 105–6.

rather substantial reasons, at least as profound as their own mistrust of Russia, and might lead the Russians to conclude a pact with Hitler. Rumours of a possible Nazi–Soviet deal were never taken seriously.

The Soviet nightmare was a German invasion of Russia, a war in which she might have to fight alone and receive the German attack on Russian soil instead of going out to meet it in the Baltic states, Poland, and Rumania. In view of Munich, there was little confidence in France and Britain. But Britain neither shared nor understood this Russian fear. Hence, Russia's demand for a direct alliance seemed irrelevant, and the Russian fear of attack through the Baltic states only an excuse for aggression. Were Russia's fears unreasonable? Only those can answer who know whether Britain would have stood by Russia to the death without the experiences of Dunkirk, the fall of France, and the London blitz.

The question whether there were any conditions on which Russia would have concluded an agreement with Britain simply cannot be answered. It seems probable that both sides wanted an agreement, but not the same agreement. Britain wanted a promise of Russian aid 'if desired'. Russia wanted a precise alliance for mutual assistance. Each move by one side increased the suspicion of the other. At the outset, Russia was probably prepared to conclude an agreement provided Britain could convince her that appeasement was dead, displaced by resolute resistance to Hitler. But she was equally prepared to pocket the immediate gains which an agreement with Germany would bring her. In the final analysis, Britain's determination to keep Russia out of Poland and the Baltic states outweighed the securing of Russian aid against Germany. Unfortunately, the British accomplished neither, salvaging only their reputation, which was of dubious practical value in the circumstances.[20]

That appeasement had not yet been laid to rest is perhaps best illustrated by the covert revival of efforts at economic appeasement in July 1939. Horace Wilson and Helmut Wohltat, the German trade commissioner, huddled in London over the possibility of a £1 billion loan to Germany. This lack of wisdom in terms of feeding Russia's suspicions, disheartening Poland, and encouraging Germany to believe that Britain was still prepared to purchase peace, is hard to exaggerate. But this 'piece of super-appeasement', as Gladwyn Jebb of the foreign office called it, shows how policies which might have had some validity several years before, if they were part of a coherent attitude towards the dictators and accompanied by a great British rearmament effort, 'were pursued relentlessly by No 10 long after it had become evident to all but the blind that Hitler was only interested in force and could only be

[20] These paragraphs rest heavily on Rock, 'Grand Alliance or Daisy Chain: British Opinion and Policy toward Russia, April–August, 1939', in Wallace and Askew (editors), *Power, Public Opinion, and Diplomacy*, pp. 330–37.

restrained, if at all, by the creating of a vast anti-Nazi coalition'.[21] Along with Chamberlain's temporizing on September 1st and 2nd, it demonstrates that appeasement retained a breath of life as long as peace remained.

This almost indestructible commitment to appeasement seems nearly impossible to understand without some reference to what might be called the psychology of appeasement. The policy originated as an open and well argued attitude. It seemed sensible, sane, the kind of charitable approach essential to friendly and productive relations among men and nations. But as the policy proved inadequate, and eventually downright erroneous, and the more it was subjected to scepticism, criticism, and at length unequivocal opposition, the more it became a passion, an obsession, which led its proponents to ignore evidence which did not fit their preconceptions (or to interpret it in strangely optimistic ways) and to look with disdain on those 'weaker' Englishmen who did not have the firm conviction of true believers. In this way, appeasement was transformed from a mood of pride and honour into one of intrigues and machinations, degenerating in both form and content in rough correlation to the brutalization of politics in those nations, especially Germany, which were its primary objects. Mesmerized by the vision of a settlement with Hitler, the advocates of appeasement imperceptibly converted their tentative hopes to pious convictions, thereby succumbing to self-deception.

The forbearance of the appeasers in the face of dictatorial threats, lies, broken promises, and rude behaviour would warrant admiration were it not for the tragic failure of their policy. Their ability to absorb disappointments and to suffer repeated insults without losing patience or faith in their purpose appears nearly abnormal. Chamberlain in particular stands out in this regard. Some of his closest colleagues were occasionally tempted to doubt and waver, to a degree in the wake of Munich, more so after Prague. But the prime minister was determined not to falter and exhibited a prickly awareness of those who did. As his desire to deal directly with the dictators had developed, so had his faith in his power to convert them to reasonable men. His mind once set on an objective, he could be a most stubborn person, his single-minded assurance and sense of personal indispensability approaching the theological sin of pride. And his influence on colleagues, a combination no doubt of respect and awe, with a heavy touch of political wisdom mixed in, was so weighty as to suggest a cult of personality in operation.[22]

That Chamberlain was able to function in this way resulted in part from the kind of men he drew around him, in part from the manner of his operation. With one or two exceptions in the period prior to Munich, Chamberlain's cabinet was made up not of bold and independent-minded persons but 'of non-entities, presided by one magisterial

[21] *The Memoirs of Lord Gladwyn*, p. 93.
[22] See Middlemas, *Diplomacy of Illusion*, pp. 449–50.

personality'.[23] Most ministers were so like-minded with Chamberlain that little critical sifting of policy occurred; and without it the prime minister became credulous, naive, and self-confident. Nor did cabinet changes ever broaden the range of opinions. That would only impede the pursuit of appeasement and possibly provoke the dictators. Yet rumblings were seldom heard from within the Conservative party or the large contingent of 'regular' Conservatives in the Commons; indeed, the latter seemed to constitute an effective body of yes-men devoted to unquestioning compliance wherever it might lead.

In these circumstances, the structure of decision-making in Chamberlain's cabinet was pyramidal, the prime minister at the top, functioning rather autocratically. He consulted his colleagues often and openly enough; but he always assumed that, with the process of reasoning thus exercised, all ministers would naturally arrive at conclusions the same as his own. Further, he sometimes determined his policy in advance, utilizing cabinet meetings to inform his colleagues of decisions already taken and to press his views upon them.[24] Thus, for example, the decision to go to Germany to talk with Hitler, the promise of a guarantee to rump Czechoslovakia, and the warning to Czechoslovakia to cede the Sudetenland were all formulated without cabinet consultation. In fact, during the crisis of September 1938, cabinet responsibility was appropriated by a small and impromptu inner circle, Chamberlain, Halifax, Hoare, and Simon, wherein there was safe consensus, and the full cabinet was reduced to the role of approving actions already accomplished. Chamberlain seldom changed his mind on a subject within the immediate context of cabinet discussion, though he sometimes shifted ground between cabinets, presumably on the basis of informal deliberation with those friends and ministers whom he chose to consult.[25]

Had there been among his friends and advisers those who were expert on the essentials of foreign policy, Chamberlain's relationship with his cabinet, which was not wholly unusual, would not necessarily have been deterimental. But expert advice, except from those who would tell him what he wanted to hear, was something he did not welcome. He had fixed his mind on what needed to be done and the manner in which he would do it. Those who objected were simply mistaken;

[23] Colvin, *The Chamberlain Cabinet*, p. 262.

[24] In order to obtain cabinet approval for the thing he wanted to do, Chamberlain sometimes offered impressions, especially about Hitler, which it is hard to imagine that he himself believed. Two examples are his heavy emphasis on Hitler's reliability, September 17th and 24th 1938, despite his own earlier, private, lamentations about the German government's utterly untrustworthy and dishonest nature and his brutal treatment by Hitler at Godesberg. Perhaps Chamberlain was fooled by Hitler; conflicting evidence makes it very hard to say. But he does not fare well in any case. If he was fooled, it would seem to reveal a lack of perception, a political myopia of very dangerous proportions. If he was not fooled, there remains a stubborn refusal to face facts and a blind adherence to wishful thinking.

[25] See Middlemas, *Diplomacy of Illusion*, pp. 315, 410, 447, *passim;* Colvin, *The Chamberlain Cabinet*, pp. 19, 264–5, *passim.*

those who urged caution were shallow and slow. All must be by-passed or simply ignored. Herein lay the critical disadvantage of Chamberlain's establishment of a private little 'foreign office' under Horace Wilson at No 10, his frequent circumventing of the regular foreign office, and his use of intermediaries, amateurs in diplomacy, to carry out his instructions. It prevented him from getting responsible advice from those whose business it was to know foreign affairs, orthodox advice, perhaps, but nonetheless useful in balancing his personal impulses. Rarely were senior civil servants invited to cabinet meetings. Seldom were they consulted outside it. Decision-making in foreign affairs was Chamberlain's personal province, 'a rigid satrapy closed against the light of opposition and informed only by the servants of appeasement'.[26]

Of British appeasement in the 1930s it must simply be said that, however worthy its aims and objectives, its style and temper were ill-suited and ill-adapted to the fascist dictators who were its objects. In their understanding of the new totalitarian forces at work in Europe, Nazism in particular, many of the leading appeasers clearly fell short. Chamberlain, for example, was convinced until he died in November 1940 that appeasement had failed largely through the unfortunate accident of his having encountered a fanatic in Hitler. The Führer was seen as a separate phenomenon rather than the symbol and spearhead of a vast new force in German life. This error of judgement helps to explain the prime minister's misplaced reliance on the restraining influence of the German people and his interest in personal, travelling diplomacy, by which he might make contact with the people in fascist countries and appeal to their peaceful instincts over the heads of their leaders.

No one can argue with certainty that a British policy other than appeasement, or that active appeasement attempted earlier, would have prevented the Second World War. The elements of chance and choice in history are sufficiently great as to make that possible. But in view of what we have come to know about Hitler and Nazism, such a fortuitous outcome seems rather unlikely. What a different policy could have done was to force the dictators to pursue their aggressive intentions in circumstances much less favourable to their military success, thus significantly altering the appeal of any war which they might consider. It could also have educated the British people more effectively to the dangers which they confronted and prepared them better to meet the scourge of war when it was finally forced upon them. Their passion for peace notwithstanding, Chamberlain appears to have under-estimated the willingness of his countrymen to accept unpleasant reality, especially during 1939. The German peril was not exposed to the British people until very late in the day, yet the magnitude and speed of German military preparations, the vast scope of German ambitions, and disturbing danger signals in Germany's behaviour

[26] Middlemas, *Diplomacy of Illusion*, p. 447.

were all well known to those in positions of leadership. With the ignorance of the public complete, the ineptness of British policy after Munich is very inadequately vindicated by the often emphasized argument about the stringently limiting effect of public opinion on the government's policy options.[27] The common and appealing defence of appeasement in terms of uniting Britain and the Commonwealth in the belief that every conceivable effort had been made to find a way of sparing Europe the ordeal of war and that no alternative remained, neglects the possibility that the same end might have been reached by other means, with greater potential for discouraging the dictators along the way.

That appeasement was as much a stepchild of British domestic politics, that 'complex of attitudes and susceptibilities which divided the left and right . . . and split them within themselves', as a reaction to the Nazi regime is a proposition of considerable importance. No student of interwar history can fail to be impressed by the troublesome internal divisions of English society, the degree to which unsolved economic and social problems absorbed the nation's attention and energy, and the uncertain vacillations in political life and attitudes which resulted therefrom. But many of the basic problems 'about what life in Britain and what Britain's place in the world should be' were not resolved by the war, and long after continued 'to bedevil both contemporary politics and the possibility of a detached consideration of the inter-war period'.[28]

The supposition lingers, especially among some British historians, that France was the root of the problem; weak and divided, she was not willing to honour her own obligations and was disposed to shift responsibility for keeping order in Europe onto Britain's shoulders. The extent to which France's debilitation conditioned British policy remains uncertain, as does the extent to which the decline of French confidence was related to Britain's refusal to accept new commitments or to identify the circumstances in which she would or would not take action. But the insularity of the leading appeasers was one of their most striking characteristics. The French were regularly summoned to London for consultation, their stated good intentions habitually challenged, and their need for reassurance, which might stimulate them to a stronger attitude, regularly ignored. Perhaps the French were deserving of nothing better, but in view of the British government's total discounting, probably rightly, of American influence in Europe's affairs, and its extreme reluctance to associate with Russia (whose readiness to participate in the larger affairs of Europe, had the British provided suitable

[27] See Rock, *Appeasement on Trial*, p. 334. Sir Arthur Salter lends weight to this view, with particular reference to the judgement of informed public critics on home defence, in *Memoirs of a Public Servant* (London, 1961), pp. 256ff.

[28] Gannon, *The British Press and Germany, 1936–1939*, p. 31. A recent volume by Maurice Cowling, *The Impact of Hitler: British Politics and British Policy, 1933–1940* (Cambridge, 1975), examines the relationship between British party politics and the conduct of foreign policy, and takes account of the strategic and financial limitations within which decisions were made.

opportunities, must remain one of the mysteries of the pre-war period), the attitude toward France reveals a rather remarkable willingness to face the rapidly changing situation in central Europe alone.

It is easy to conclude from a study of British appeasement in the 1930s that appeasement is a policy of weakness, dishonour, and degradation which has no place in modern diplomacy. But this is to overinterpret an apparent lesson of history in terms of distorted meaning. Appeasement in the sense of the surrender of vital interests, compelled by weakness, is surely to be avoided. But appeasement in its original meaning of reasonable concessions made from a position of strength, in the interest of removing international difficulties and solidifying peace, is compatible with the highest canons of civilized relationships. Given the human proclivity to generalize from the specific, especially with regard to bad experiences, it may never be possible to restore the term appeasement to its original meaning. But the original idea of appeasement, by whatever name it is known, is still a fundamental purpose of diplomacy, an essential and sometimes invaluable card in an on-going game which should not be discarded antipathetically because it was once misplayed, in the wrong circumstances and against the wrong opponent, in a crucial contest more than a generation ago. Charges of 'appeasement', for the purpose of condemnation, levelled against a policy which aims at easing tension and avoiding conflict are hardly appropriate at a time when all-out war, because of its very nature, is no longer a feasible instrument of policy even for aggressive, expansionist powers. And stigmatizing as 'appeasement' policies of balancing and adjustment misses the mark entirely in a world where such policies are the only means of assuring peaceful coexistence, and peaceful competition, among antagonistic blocs and systems.[29]

Of course, there are certain qualifications which must be acknowledged. Appeasement should always be implemented from a position of strength. If peace-loving powers become so weak that, individually or collectively, by means of alliance or other arrangements, they cannot confidently and effectively stand up to potential aggressors, they are courting disaster. There must be a broad appreciation of vital interests, including recognition that the most vital of all, a people's way of life, may be threatened by developments farther afield than is often at first perceived. Decisions on matters of this kind are among the most difficult in diplomacy, but a narrow, isolationist view in the closely interrelated world of the present is both dangerous and foolhardy. There must be early signs that the object of appeasement is appeasable. Appeasement has a rightful place in resolving disputes through negotiated settlement and peaceful change; but it is wholly inappropriate in dealing with force, violence, and aggression. Concessions made by a

---

[29] See Herz, 'The Relevancy and Irrelevancy of Appeasement', p. 320. Herz identifies three basic factors which fundamentally differentiate more recent conditions from those of the 1930s (pp. 309ff).

government should never involve the surrender of fundamental principles upon the preservation of which the claim to loyalty and respect for that government depends. That would constitute betrayal, by the means, of the very ends which they were devised to defend and promote.[30]

This connotes a matter of values and morals, one of the thorniest aspects of appeasement evaluation. It is well to recognize forthrightly that value theory and ethical standards are as much a part of the historical evaluation of appeasement as the delineation of national interests or assessments of intent and power. The appeasers of the 1930s came to appear immoral, both to some contemporary opponents and later critics, partly because they were too easily inclined to risk national interests, partly because they placed in jeopardy the balance of power system on which Britain traditionally relied for security, but particularly because they were ready to bargain over the freedom from fascist control of individuals, groups, and nations, even to make it a matter of unilateral concession.[31] These matters necessarily involve judgements of political morality and are therefore subject to varying interpretations.

Indeed, the extent to which appeasement can be held responsible for German aggression and the outbreak of the Second World War is not simply a matter of historical fact. It involves an issue of ethical judgement, the crux of which is readily seen through the use of a simple analogy. When a person stubbornly or naively travels a dark street on a mission of mercy or goodwill, even though warned to avoid it for reasons of personal danger, the responsibility for any attack which occurs may be debated. There are some who would fault the traveller for encouraging the potential assailant by giving him the opportunity to practice his 'art'. There are those who would fault the assailant for his shocking, aggressive, however premediated, behaviour. Chamberlain was a traveller walking time and again on Hitler's street for the purpose of seeking appeasement, a worthy objective by any normal standard of measure. Hitler was the waiting and anxious assailant, at first inclined to robbery and later intent on murder. If traditional western values have any meaning at all, it should not be too difficult to decide which must bear basic and final responsibility for the struggle that eventually resulted. The wisdom of appeasement, particularly in its later stages, is certainly open to question, but its ethical objectives are not. The same can hardly be said for Nazi policy. As Alan Bullock has convincingly put it, the appeasers' share of the responsibility for the war is that

> they were reluctant to recognize what was happening, reluctant to give a lead in opposing it, reluctant to act in time. Hitler understood their state of mind perfectly and played on it with skill. None of the Great Powers comes out well in the history of the 1930s, but

---

[30] See Wheeler-Bennett, *Munich: Prologue to Tragedy*, pp. 7–8.
[31] Middlemas sees as the guiding assumption of Chamberlain's political philosophy 'that men would rather be unfree and alive than free but tormented or dead'. *Diplomacy of Illusion*, p. 256.

this sort of responsibility even when it runs to appeasement . . .
is still recognizably different from that of a government [Hitler's]
which deliberately creates the threat of war and sets out to exploit
it.[32]

Britain, and Europe, were vastly changed after the appeasement era.
The first generation of Britain's post-war history was consumed by
efforts to adjust to a position of gradually decreasing power, consisting
in the main of withdrawal from exposed positions in the world, abandonment of the role of a prime mover in world affairs, and the acceptance of
interdependence with western Europe.[33] Climaxed by the tremendous
impact of the war itself, appeasement was both cause and symptom of
Britain's decline. It was a kind of prelude to momentous change in
Britain's world position which is still today unfolding.

---

[32] Quoted in Louis,, *The Origins of the Second World War*, p. 145.
[33] This is the central theme of a recent study by Joseph Frankel, *British Foreign Policy, 1945–1973* (London, 1975).

Bibliography

Since the action taken in the late 1960s to reduce from fifty to thirty years the period of time after which most official British records are open to the public, several important studies of the latter segment of the appeasement era have appeared, among them, Keith Middlemas, *Diplomacy of Illusion: the British Government and Germany, 1937–1939* (London, 1972), and Ian Colvin, *The Chamberlain Cabinet* (London, 1971). Concentrating on policy formulation within the cabinet, these revealing works are basic to a study of appeasement during Chamberlain's premiership. Other notable works which utilize the official records in different ways include Maurice Cowling, *The Impact of Hitler: British Politics and British Policy, 1933–1940* (Cambridge and New York, 1975); J. W. Bruegel, *Czechoslovakia before Munich: The German Minority Problem and British Appeasement Policy* (Cambridge, 1973); Sidney Aster, *1939: the Making of the Second World War* (New York, 1973); and Roger Parkinson, *Peace For Our Time: Munich to Dunkirk—the Inside Story* (New York, 1971).

Numerous works which appeared before 1970 on various aspects of appeasement remain valuable. Martin Gilbert and Richard Gott, *The Appeasers* (London, 1963) describes what the appeasers sought and the methods they were prepared to use to attain their ends. In *The Roots of Appeasement* (London, 1966), Martin Gilbert traces the historical antecedents of the policy and shows that it was a noble idea rooted in Christianity, courage, and common sense. On the other hand, A. L. Rowse excoriates the leading appeasers in his brief polemic *Appeasement: a Study in Political Decline* (New York, 1961), while Margaret George probes their motives, particularly the issue of (economic) class prejudice, in *The Warped Vision: British Foreign Policy, 1933–1939* (Pittsburgh, 1965). W. N. Medlicott shows Anglo-German efforts toward an understanding before 1938 in *Britain and Germany: the Search for Agreement, 1930–1937* (London, 1969). Opposition to appeasement, particularly in parliament and press, is examined in William R. Rock, *Appeasement on Trial: British Foreign Policy and its Critics, 1938–1939* (Hamden, 1966), while Neville Thompson treats one significant segment of the opposition in *The Anti-Appeasers: Conservative Opposition to Appeasement in the 1930s* (Oxford, 1971). The appeasement-related attitudes of ten leading newspapers in the late 1930s are traced in Franklin R. Gannon, *The British Press and Germany, 1936–1939* (Oxford, 1971).

Among a variety of works on broader subjects which include extensive material on, and evaluations of, British appeasement, the following are noteworthy: F. S. Northedge, *The Troubled Giant: Britain among the Great Powers, 1916–1939* (London and New York, 1966); A. J. P. Taylor, *The Origins of the Second World War* (London, 1961); Christopher Thorne, *The Approach of War, 1938–1939* (London, 1967); and Laurence Lafore, *The End of Glory: an Inter-*

pretation of the Origins of World War II (Philadelphia, 1970). Also useful are pertinent sections of D. C. Watt, *Personalities and Policies: Studies in the Formulation of British Foreign Policy in the Twentieth Century* (Notre Dame, 1965); Charles L. Mowat, *Britain between the Wars 1918–1940*(Chicago, 1955; London, 1968); A. J. P. Taylor, *English History, 1914–1945* (Oxford and New York, 1965); Ian Colvin, *Vansittart in Office: an Historical Survey of the Origins of the Second World War Based on the Papers of Sir Robert Vansittart* (London, 1965); *The History of The Times* IV, part 2 (New York, 1952); L. B. Namier, *Diplomatic Prelude, 1938–1939* (London, 1948); L. B. Namier, *Europe in Decay: a Study in Disintegration, 1936–1940* (London, 1950); and pertinent volumes in the *Survey of International Affairs*, edited by Arnold Toynbee.

British policy between the wars, with particular reference to her relationship with France and her attitude towards Germany, is treated in two old but useful volumes: Arnold Wolfers, *Britain and France between Two Wars: Conflicting Strategies of Peace Since Versailles* (New York, 1940), and W. M. Jordan, *Great Britain, France, and the German Problem* (London, 1943). Anglo-French relations, with particular reference to appeasement, are assessed in Arthur H. Furnia, *The Diplomacy of Appeasement: Anglo-French Relations and the Prelude to World War II, 1931–1938* (Washington, 1960), which is somewhat too kind toward France, and sections of Neville Waites (editor) *Troubled Neighbours: Franco-British Relations in the Twentieth Century* (New York, 1966). Peter Dennis, *Decision by Default: Peacetime Conscription and British Defence, 1919–1939* (Durham, 1972) illuminates the impact of defence considerations on foreign policy. The fullest treatment of economic appeasement thus far is Berndt Jürgen Wendt, *Economic Appeasement: Handel und Finanz in der britischen Deutschland Politik, 1933–1939* (Düsseldorf, 1971). British policy in East Asia and its relationship to European appeasement is detailed in Bradford A. Lee, *Britain and the Sino-Japanese War, 1937–1939: A Study in the Dilemmas of British Decline* (Stanford, 1973). Ann Trotter, *Britain and East Asia, 1933–1937* (New York, 1975) deals with earlier years.

A few biographies of leading figures who were associated in one way or another with the appeasement era are deserving of mention: R. K. Middlemas and A. J. L. Barnes, *Baldwin* (London, 1969); G. M. Young, *Stanley Baldwin* (London, 1952); Keith Feiling, *The Life of Neville Chamberlain* (London, 1947); Iain Macleod, *Neville Chamberlain* (London, 1961), William R. Rock, *Neville Chamberlain* (New York, 1969); The earl of Birkenhead, *Halifax: the Life of Lord Halifax* (London, 1965); John Evelyn Wrench, *Geoffrey Dawson and Our Times* (London, 1955); and J. R. M. Butler, *Lord Lothian* (London, 1960). Numerous 'interim' biographies of Churchill and Eden may be consulted with some profit.

Munich has been the subject of a large number of studies which relate to appeasement more broadly. John W. Wheeler-Bennett, *Munich: Prologue to Tragedy* (London, 1948) is dated but still considered 'standard'. Others of note are Keith Eubank, *Munich* (Norman, 1963); Keith Robbins, *Munich, 1938* (London, 1968); Andrew Rothstein, *The Munich Conspiracy* (London, 1958); Boris Celovsky, *Das Münchener Abkommen von 1938* (Stuttgart, 1958); Donald Lammers, *Explaining Munich: the Search for Motive in British Policy* (Stanford, 1966); Henri Noguères, *Munich: 'Peace For Our Time'* (London, 1963); and Laurence Thompson, *The Greatest Treason: the Untold Story of Munich* (New York, 1968).

The most useful materials for conveying the flavour of both pro-appeasement and anti-appeasement attitudes are the memoirs, diaries, and papers of leading figures. These vary greatly in depth of content and consequent utility, but taken together, and consulted with circumspection, they are quite revealing. The case for appeasement is perhaps best set forth in Viscount Templewood (Sir Samuel Hoare), *Nine Troubled Years* (London, 1954). Sir Nevile Henderson, *Failure of a Mission: Berlin, 1937–1939* (New York, 1940); Lord Butler, *The Art of the Possible: the Memoirs of Lord Butler* (London, 1971); *In Search of Peace* (New York, 1939), collected speeches of Neville Chamberlain; and H. H. E. Craster (editor), *Speeches on Foreign Policy by Viscount Halifax* (London, 1940) are also valuable in this connection, as are Thomas Jones, *A Diary with Letters, 1931–1950* (London, 1954) and David Dilks (editor), *The Diaries of Sir Alexander Cadogan, 1938–1945* (London, 1971). Lord Halifax, *Fullness of Days* (New York, 1957) and Sir John Simon, *Retrospect: the Memoirs of the Right Honourable Viscount Simon* (London, 1952) are thin. The case against appeasement as seen by dissident Conservatives emerges from Winston S. Churchill, *The Gathering Storm* (London and Boston, 1948); Churchill's collected speeches, *Step by Step, 1936–1939* (New York, 1939); the earl of Avon, *The Memoirs of Anthony Eden: Facing the Dictators* (London and Boston, 1962) and *The Reckoning* (London and Boston, 1965); Eden's collected speeches, *Foreign Affairs* (New York, 1939); Duff Cooper, *Old Men Forget: the Autobiography of Duff Cooper* (London, 1953); L. S. Amery, *My Political Life* III (London, 1955); Harold Macmillan, *Winds of Change, 1914–1939* (London and New York, 1966); and Harold Nicolson, *Diaries and Letters, 1930–1939* (London, 1967). The Labour view appears in Hugh Dalton, *The Fateful Years, Memoirs, 1931–1945* (London, 1957), and to a much lesser extent in Clement Attlee, *As It Happened* (New York, 1954). Viscount Samuel, *Memoirs* (London, 1945) offers the Liberal viewpoint. From vantage points in the foreign office, in addition to the Cadogan diaries, John Harvey (editor), *The Diplomatic Diaries of Oliver Harvey, 1937–1940* (London, 1970); Lord Strang, *Home and Abroad* (London, 1956); and *The Memoirs of Lord Gladwyn* (New York, 1972) are noteworthy. On the military side, Roderick Macleod and Denis Kelly (editors) *The Ironside Diaries, 1937–1940* (London, 1962); Brian Bond (editor), *Chief of Staff: the Diaries of Lieutenant-General Sir Henry Pownall* I (Hamden, 1973); R. J. Minney (editor), *The Private Papers of Hore-Belisha* (New York, 1961); and *The Liddell Hart Memoirs* (2 vols, New York, 1965) are useful.

Of value among the memoirs of some prominent non-Englishmen are: Georges Bonnet (French foreign minister), *Défense de la Paix* (2 vols, Geneva, 1946, 1948), which must be read with caution; Herbert von Dirksen (German ambassador in London), *Moscow, Tokyo, London: Twenty Years of German Foreign Policy* (Norman, 1952); Ivan Maisky (Russian ambassador in London), *Who Helped Hitler?* (London, 1964); Robert Coulondre (French ambassador in Moscow and Berlin), *De Staline à Hitler: souvenirs de deux ambassades, 1936–1939* (Paris, 1950); and André Francois-Poncet (French ambassador in Berlin), *The Fateful Years, 1931–1938* (New York, 1949).

Among many provocative articles on appeasement, three are of special note here: D. C. Watt, 'Appeasement: the Rise of a Revisionist School?' *Political Quarterly* XXXVI, 2 (1965), which reviews the first generation of scholarship on appeasement and points to future directions; Edward Whiting Fox, 'Munich and Peace for *Our* Time?' *Virginia Quarterly Review* XL, no. 1 (1964), a stimulating reassessment of Munich and appeasement on its twenty-fifth anniversary; and

John H. Herz, 'The Relevancy and Irrelevancy of Appeasement', *Social Research* xxxi, no. 3 (1964), which discusses the validity of appeasement as a technique of foreign policy in the bipolar world of the 1960s. Other useful articles, with titles which generally describe their subject area, include: C. A. MacDonald, 'Economic Appeasement and the German "Moderates", 1937–1939: an Introductory Essay', *Past and Present*, no. 56 (August, 1972); Donald Watt, 'Roosevelt and Chamberlain: Two Appeasers', *International Journal* xxviii, no. 2 (1973); William R. Rock, 'The British Guarantee to Poland, March, 1939: a Problem in Diplomatic Decision-making', *South Atlantic Quarterly* lxv, no. 2 (1966); C. A. MacDonald, 'Britain, France, and the April Crisis of 1939', *European Studies Review* ii, no. 2 (1972); William E. Scott, 'Neville Chamberlain and Munich: Two Aspects of Power', in Leonard Krieger and Fritz Stern (editors), *The Responsibility of Power* (New York, 1967); and Sidney Aster, 'Ivan Maisky and Parliamentary Anti-Appeasement, 1938–1939', in A. J. P. Taylor (editor), *Lloyd George: Twelve Essays* (London, 1971).

Primary material of greatest importance is contained in the many volumes of *Documents on British Foreign Policy, 1919–1939; Documents on German Foreign Policy, 1918–1945; Parliamentary Debates: House of Commons*, fifth series; and in the foreign office and cabinet records located in the Public Record Office in London.

Index

This study provides, first, an explanation of the political, economic, and military factors that prompted the evolution of a policy designed above all to safeguard European peace by the progressive alleviation of German grievances arising from the Versailles settlement, but subsequently inflamed by Hitler. Secondly, it exhibits a sympathetic and informed understanding of the collective antiwar mentality of the British people, at a time of postwar disillusionment, contracting economic horizons, waning international influence, and the anticipated complete vulnerability of the civilian population to German air attack. Thirdly, the author gives a fair but clinical estimate of Neville Chamberlain's own personal responsibility, as prime minister, for the original conception of the policy of "active" appeasement and his stubborn adherence to it in the face of repeated setbacks and tragic failures.

William R. Rock is professor of history at Bowling Green State University.